The NOACH Project

THE NOACH PROJECT

Navigating the Path of *The Seven Noahide Laws*:
Stories, Key Lessons, and Resources.

LEBA BAT NOAH

Publisher's Cataloging-in-Publication Data

Names: Noah, Leba bat, author.
Title: The NOACH project : navigating the path of the seven Noahide laws : stories , key lessons , and resources / Leba bat Noah.
Description: Includes bibliographical references. | Or Noach Press, 2025.
Identifiers: LCCN: 2025918150 | ISBN: 979-8-9855221-3-6 (hardcover) | 979-8-9855221-2-9 (paperback) | 979-8-9855221-4-3 (ebook)
Subjects: LCSH Noah, Leba bat. | Noahide Laws. | Noahides. | Spiritual biography. | BISAC RELIGION / Judaism / Theology | RELIGION / Spirituality | BIOGRAPHY & AUTOBIOGRAPHY / Religious | RELIGION / Judaism / History | RELIGION / Comparative Religion
Classification: LCC BM520.73 .B38 2025 | DDC 296.36--dc23

Printed in the United States of America

For information, contact:
Leba bat Noah
TheNoachProject@gmail.com

"They will not harm nor destroy on all My holy mountain,
for the earth will be filled with the knowledge of G-d
as water covers the seabed."

–Isaiah 11:9

TABLE OF CONTENTS

PREFACE

The Seven Noahide Commandments: A Universal Moral Code

The Seven Noahide Commandments, also known as the Noahide Laws, are a set of eternal commandments and a system of ethical principles that apply for all of humanity. Rooted in *Genesis*, they serve as a universal moral framework, guiding non-Jews in leading lives that are righteous in G-d's eyes. According to the Oral Torah tradition, they were all given by G-d to Noah after the Great Flood, for all his descendants.

They can be briefly summarized as follows, but each one includes many details and logical extensions:

1. **Do not worship idols.**
   Acknowledging and worshiping only the One G-d.
2. **Do not blaspheme G-d's name.**
   Speaking about G-d with reverence and taking care not to disrespect or curse Him.
3. **Do not murder.**
   Taking a human life can not be justified unless it is sanctioned within G-d's Laws, for we are all created in His image.
4. **Do not steal.**
   Respecting the property and rights of others.

5. **Do not commit sexual transgressions.**
   Upholding family and societal integrity by rejecting adultery, incest, and other forbidden relationships.
6. **Do not eat meat that was removed from a living animal.**
   Observing this dietary law is also a reminder not to be cruel to any living creatures.
7. **Establish just laws and courts.**
   Upholding righteous and beneficial laws, and courts that maintain law and order with judicial integrity.

These commandments form the foundation of a just and ethical civilization. The Oral Torah tradition teaches that non-Jews who follow the Noahide Laws are considered righteous and worthy of special spiritual reward in their afterlife, and that those who furthermore observe them carefully as their commandments from the Torah of Moses will also have a share in the future eternal World to Come.[1]

The Seven Noahide Laws are discussed in Talmudic and subsequent rabbinical writings, as a distinct category within the Torah Law. Some of the key sources include:

- ***Genesis 2:16*** and ***2:24.*** Relates that the one G-d communicated commandments to human beings from the beginning of their creation.
- ***Genesis 9:1-17.*** Describes G-d's covenant with Noah and his descendants after the great flood, beginning with the re-establishment of a Divine moral code for humanity.

1. See *Seven Gates of Righteous Knowledge*, the Seventh Gate, chs. 3, 4, 7 and 8 in the printed edition.

- ***Talmud, Sanhedrin 56a-60a.*** Defines the specific Seven Noahide Laws, before going into discussions and debates of possible extensions into other areas. In contrast, compilation of the Torah laws that non-Jews are to obligated observe in practice was begun by Maimonides in *Laws of Kings,* chapters 9-10 (see below).
- ***Midrash Genesis Rabbah 34:8.*** Defines the specific Seven Noahide Laws, along with a list of possible extensions into other areas.
- ***Maimonides (Rambam), Mishneh Torah, Laws of Kings (Hilchot Melachim) 9-10.*** Chapter 9 gives a concise description of the Seven Noahide Laws along with some additional source verses, and outlines their role in the moral and legal Torah-law framework for non-Jews. Chapter 10 provides more details, as well as information on the obligatory boundaries between the observances of Jews and non-Jews.

Together, these sources prove that the Seven Noahide Laws for non-Jews were included by G-d in the Written and Oral Torah that was given through Moses. They offer a timeless Divine moral code that is meant to foster a world built on justice, respect, and ethical responsibility.

Since the early 1980s, a steadily increasing number of people around the world are actively following these principles as the basis of their spiritual faith. They commonly refer to themselves alternatively as Noachides[2], Noahides, or *Bnei Noach* (Hebrew for "Children of Noah").

---

2. First used in modern times by Rabbi Elijah Benamozegh, in *Israël et l'humanité*, pub. 1914.

On the names G-d and Hashem, and scriptural terminology:

Throughout this book, you will notice that the Creator is most often referred to in English as "G-d". The written word is hyphenated due to reverence and respect. This follows the Jewish tradition of not writing His name spelled out in full, if it might be erased, discarded, or treated casually.

You will also see the name "Hashem" used interchangeably for "G-d". Literally, "Hashem" means "The Name" in Hebrew. This is another proper and respectful way to refer to G-d without using a sanctified holy name, and it is used by many Noahides. Whether we use the names G-d or Hashem, we speak of the one Creator, our Guide, our Source of life, and the One we strive to know and serve.

In addition, some interviewees refer to the "Old Testament" and "New Testament" as part of recounting their personal journeys. These names are familiar to those who have come from Christian backgrounds. Because these terms reflect the language and experiences of those sharing their stories, I chose not to alter their wording, allowing their voices to remain authentic to their lived experiences. Ultimately, this book seeks to honor the sincerity and courage of those who have chosen to follow G-d's path of the Noahide Laws, wherever their journeys began.

In contrast, the authentic 24 Books of the Hebrew Bible (*Genesis* through *Chronicles*), which are also the holy scriptures for Noahides, are referred to in Hebrew as the "Tanach".[3]

---

3. The *Tanach* (also spelled *Tanakh)* is the Hebrew Bible, composed of three sections: the *Torah* (Five Books of Moses), *Nevi'im* (Prophets), and *Chetuvim* (Writings). The name is derived from the initials T–N–Ch.

What's in a name? About the use of "ben Noah" and "bat Noah":

As you read through this book, you'll notice that some of the Noahides are listed with their given names, along with "ben Noah" for a man, or "bat Noah" for a woman. In Hebrew, bat Noah means "daughter of Noah," and ben Noah means "son of Noah." These are titles that many Noahides use to express their connection to this path. Others are identified by their full name, and some have chosen a Hebrew first name as well.

Each featured person made a thoughtful choice about how to be named in this book. For some, the use of ben Noah or bat Noah reflects their identity and values. For others, their given name or Hebrew name holds special meaning. Names are deeply personal, and in a project like this, where people are sharing something so meaningful, how they choose to be known is part of their story.

ACKNOWLEDGEMENTS

I am so very grateful to all who helped bring *The NOACH Project* to life.

To **Dr. Michael Schulman**, thank you for your invaluable guidance in consulting and editing. Who better to advise on a book about the Seven Noahide Laws than the Director of Ask Noah International, publisher and editor of *The Divine Code*. Your time, direction, and wisdom have been a great help throughout this project, and I am also grateful for the introductions you made to several Noahides who added their voices to this work.

To **Rabbi Lazer Brody**, I am especially grateful for your generosity in connecting me with so many Noahides whose stories became part of this book. Your support made it possible to include voices that brought depth, diversity, and richness to the project.

To **Rabbi** and **Rebbetzin Feldman**, thank you for welcoming me so warmly into your congregation. Through your guidance and kindness, and within the community you are building, I have found a place where I can learn, connect, and discover deeper meaning in life through Torah. For this sense of home, inspiration, and connection, I am so grateful.

To **Hannah, Daniel, Boaz, Judith, Fumani, Channah Elanna Hadassah, Daisy, Stefan, Samuel, Eliana, Justin, Melissa, Jecinta, Fred, Anne Marie, Eliyahu, Nancy, Craig, Jennifer, Katy, Jim, Sebastian,** and **Pamela...** this book exists because of you. Thank you for trusting me with your stories, for opening your hearts, and for showing the world what it means to live as a Noahide. Your courage and honesty are the soul of *The NOACH Project.*

To **my husband**, who "just happened" to pull the Chumash off the shelf and set everything in motion. That moment sparked our learning and gave us a shared language, one that's brought us closer to each other and to G-d.

To **my friends**, who encouraged me, who showed curiosity about this project, who cheered me on, and who supported this vision from the very beginning.

Above all, my deepest thanks go to **Hashem**, for revealing this extraordinary path. It is at once puzzling and delightful, and most of all, a source of deep gratitude.

INTRODUCTION

"Not all those who wander are lost."

–The Riddle of Strider. J.R.R. Tolkien

This book shares the stories of ordinary people who are not so ordinary after all. There is nothing typical about choosing the Noahide path. What motivates people around the world to step away from the religion they were raised in, to walk away from the culture they were born into, and instead embrace the one G-d, the G-d of Israel? That kind of decision takes courage. But it also takes vision, the ability to imagine a different kind of life, one shaped by meaning, self-development, and connection. The people you'll meet in these pages are seekers. Most of them had far more questions than answers about the religious path they were on, and their efforts to find clarity within their own tradition often led to dead ends. It was only when they turned to the original source, the Hebrew Bible, that things began to make sense.

The idea for this book formed through many conversations with fellow Noahides. Again and again, I heard similar themes. People spoke about the beauty of the path, but also its challenges, what it means to step outside of the mainstream, to live in a space between cultures, and to seek G-d without a feeling of fully belonging anywhere. Many described the grief of lost friendships, the strain on family relationships, and the complexity of raising children with values that don't always match the world around them.

These stories made it clear that there was a need for a space like this, a place where people who revere the G-d of Israel and want to live as the "righteous among the nations" could be acknowledged, heard, and understood.

One feeling I heard expressed often was the experience of not quite belonging. Not in the religion or culture that was left behind, and not fully among the Jewish people either. Some, however, have found places of connection and support. That has been true for me. I feel incredibly grateful to be part of the Chabad Jewish community in my town, where the Rabbi and Rebbetzin have welcomed me with kindness, respect, and inclusion. Being invited into classes and celebrations has given me the opportunity to grow in my understanding of the principles of Jewish *emuna*[4] and deepen my relationship with G-d, as I have come to know of Him as *Hashem*[5].

This path is one of ongoing learning. It is not always easy. There are moments of doubt, mistakes, and awkward steps forward. Those are when the principles of *bitachon*[6] become so important. It is *bitachon* that gives clarity, insight, and a growing sense of what it means to live with integrity and awareness. Every step is part of the process.

Jewish tradition teaches that the Torah is the blueprint of creation. While Noahides are not Jews, the Divine wisdom of Torah speaks to all of humanity. In times of confusion, fear, or transition, it offers stability, purpose, and direction.

This book is a collection of honest voices. Some tell stories of struggle and transformation. Others reflect on moments of deep

4. *Emuna* (or *emunah*) is the word in Hebrew for "faith", and most specifically, faith in the one G-d and His Torah.
5. The use of this Hebrew term to refer to G-d was explained in the Preface.
6. *Bitachon* is the word in Hebrew for "trust", and most specifically, trust in G-d.

realization and personal growth. What they all share is a deep love for the one G-d, the G-d of Israel, and a sincere commitment to living meaningful lives.

If you are already walking this path, may these stories strengthen and uplift you.

If you are just beginning, or contemplating beginning, may they remind you that you are not alone. Because truly, you are not.

Leba bat Noah

APPROBATIONS

בס"ד

Rabbi Eliezer Raphael ("Lazer") Brody
Mashpia Ruchni (Spiritual Advisor)

Author of *13 Principles of Emuna, 3 Words of Emuna, Bitachon, Divine Direction, The Bond of Emuna, The Serene Soul, Emuna and the Noahide, Path to Your Peak,* and other books.

בעהמ"ח ספר פי הבאר עה"ת, נפשי תדום

B"H, 13 Nissan, 5785 (10 April, 2025)

I am delighted to recommend a very special and heartwarming book, *The NOACH Project*, by Leba Bat Noah. This book is a refreshing compendium of the personal experiences of a select group of people from around the world, many of whom I have met and know personally.

The lovely aspect about *The NOACH Project*, is the way it shows how each remarkably unique individual navigated his or her extraordinary path in discovering truth and developing a deep love for the G-d of Israel.

This book is a drink of cool water for the spiritually-parched throats that are searching for meaning in life and true spirituality.

May the Almighty bless the author with success in all of her endeavors.

With prayers for the long-awaited day when all of living flesh shall call out to Hashem, thus hastening the imminent redemption with the rebuilding of our Holy Temple in Jerusalem,

Eliezer Raphael (Lazer) Brody,
Director of Emuna Beams Outreach, EmunaBeams.com
Ashdod, Land of Israel

בס״ד

I congratulate our friend Leba bat Noah on the compilation of *The NOACH Project* with great joy and appreciation for her work, and for the willingness of all participants to be a part of it. What Leba and her participants have done is give the reader a window on the lives of brave spiritual seekers who, like "Abraham, My friend" (*Isaiah 41:8*), have often left familiarity, comfort and support in search of truth and a genuine relationship with Hashem. Finding myself in the presence of such incredible people, it was truly humbling to be asked to provide an endorsement for the book.

One of the most important aspects of this book is the "Key Lessons" section that appears at the end of each personal entry. Here, the reader can glean insights and guidance for his or her own journey and reflect upon how these match his or her own experience. This section provides an almanac of sorts, an heirloom from fellow travelers which can be very valuable to the reader.

Common to most peoples' personal account is an acknowledgement of the real human challenge of isolation, something that many people who walk the Noahide path experience. The Torah's vision for humanity is one that ultimately sees all of us as one community, as the verse states, "For then I will convert the peoples to a purer language, that they may all call upon the name of the L-rd, to serve Him with one consent" (*Zephaniah 3:9*). However, sociological research has demonstrated that once a community exceeds a certain number people, less connection is felt between its members. For this reason, we at Sukkat Shalom-Bnei Noach have endeavored to create an interactive, spiritual community of friends and families to grow together.

What Leba and her co-authors have done is also essential to alleviating this challenge through the development of materials that build connection between people and uphold the integrity of the Torah's covenant with humanity. I respectfully submit my approbation for *The NOACH Project.* The verse in Psalms 84:8 states, "They go from strength to strength; every one of them appears before God in Zion." Blessings to Leba bat Noah and the others, that they "go from strength to strength" and continue to make this world a brighter and warmer place through their good works.

Bivracha, (*with blessings*)
Tanchum Shlomo Burton

Jerusalem Lights

Elul 9, 5785 – September 2, 2025

We are immensely fortunate to have Leba bat Noah's sensitive and inspiring book, *The NOACH Project*.

The pages of this book are filled with stories of the personal journeys of individuals from all over the world, and from all walks of life, who have sought out a relationship with the One G-d of Israel. These are people of great integrity and sincerity, who have chosen to live their lives according to the authentic Torah values that G-d bequeathed to all humanity through the Noahide covenant. The life lessons they share in these pages exude great faith, vision and dedication, and testify to the global spiritual revolution that we are witnessing today, manifest as a great yearning for G-d and foreseen by the prophet Amos (8:11): "Behold, days are coming, says Hashem G-d, when I will send a hunger over the land; not hunger for bread, or a thirst for water, but to hear the words of Hashem."

This book speaks directly to the soul of our generation, and its pages are like signposts along the road to the promised Redemption of all mankind. Our generation of spiritual seekers are active participants in this process of Redemption, of which King David prophetically foretold, (*Psalms 24:6*) "This is the generation of those who seek Him, who seek Your presence, selah."

I sincerely hope that those searching for the contemporary meaning of the eternal Torah's universal path of the Noahide covenant will avail themselves of this work. I wholeheartedly recommend *The NOACH Project* and wish Leba bat Noah every success in spreading the knowledge and light of Hashem. May Hashem bless her endeavor and may we all merit to stand together in the rebuilt Holy Temple, speedily!

Sincerely,
Rabbi Chaim Richman,

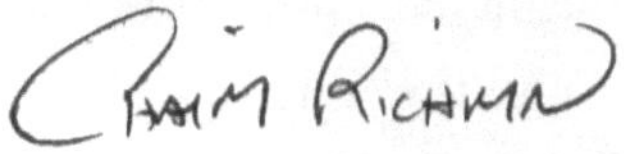

Director, Jerusalem Lights
www.RabbiRichman.com
P.O. Box 23808
Jerusalem, Israel

DISCLAIMER

Today's on-line environment is an unregulated forum of opinions and ideas. Therefore, every Noahide and anyone with a sincere interest in the Noahide movement should be diligent in seeking out expert and reliable sources of information and guidance that are true to the teachings of practical halacha (Torah law) as it applies for Jews and non-Jews, respectively.

Throughout this book, the interviewed Noahides mentioned numerous rabbis, teachers, advisors, organizations, on-line communities, websites, books and video channels. All of these were retained as being part of each individual's personal journey on the Noahide path. This does not constitute a blanket endorsement of all the resources that were named.

PERSONAL STORIES

1.

Hannah bat Noah | (Belgium)

A JOURNEY INTO JEWISH WISDOM

"I discovered that true love is about giving, not just taking. The Hebrew word for love, ahava, is rooted in the Hebrew word for 'to give.' That changed everything for me."

1. What is your background?

I was born into a family marked by many internal struggles. Both of my parents came from deeply religious backgrounds, my father from a big Protestant family and my mother from a large Catholic family. Both families had their share of difficulties, much of which was kept secret from me. My parents faced so many personal traumas and hardships that they waited five years before feeling stable enough to have a child. I was their first, and from the very beginning, there was a lot of tension between them.

My father was a strict and somewhat self-righteous Protestant. My mother's family had already left the Catholic Church, disillusioned by its failings, and converted to Protestantism, almost as an act of defiance. My mother followed her own mother (my grandmother) into the Protestant church, where my father's family had been among the founding members. But soon they found out that their hope for betterment was short-lived. That's why my father started searching for something more effective and helpful, and explored various small religious groups, J.'s Witnesses, and Mormons, before finally settling in a Pentecostal evangelical church. He chose that church because they specialized in exorcisms.

He believed my mother, who had suffered childhood trauma, was possessed. Of course, as a child, I had no understanding of this. But one of my earliest memories of how religion shaped my life happened when I went to the store with my mother and found a fairy tale book about Aladdin. I asked her to buy it for me, and she did. That evening, around five o'clock, she was reading it to me when my father unexpectedly came home early. The moment he heard her reading about spirits coming out of a lamp, he became furious. He raged that such things were dangerous and should never be read to a child. What followed was an explosive confrontation; my father, in a fit of anger, accused my mother of leading me astray, and the book was thrown into the fireplace. And this was just one incident among many.

Experiencing something like that as a child leaves a deep impression. I learned early on that my mother was "wrong," that she read the "wrong books," that she didn't recognize the supposed dangers of the demonic realm. It had a profound effect on me. From that moment, I became both intensely drawn to books and very curious about what went on in the minds of adults. We lived in isolation, in a house in the middle of nowhere, completely cut off from the world. The outside world was seen as corrupt and dangerous, so we had no television, no telephone, and no newspapers.

Over time, my mother became deeply unhappy. When my sister was born, we moved to a village, which provided some relief, but the tensions between my parents never truly faded. My childhood fascination took on two forms: books became my escape, and I became obsessed with understanding what drove the adults around me. My parents both came from large families, and at gatherings, I would make myself invisible, sit quietly, listening, trying to make sense of the complex world of grown-ups. I became incredibly sensitive to the struggles of those around me, absorbing the pain and sorrow I witnessed.

I truly believed that our church, with its full evangelical gospel, would bring healing and solutions. So I prayed fervently, for my parents, for my family, for everyone. But instead of seeing things improve, I only saw them worsen. My parents were genuinely looking for help in church to improve their lives, but the more they went to church, the more strife came into the house. I was profoundly marked by the suffering that surrounded me. It felt as though all the pain, continuous ego-fights, rivalry, suspicion and sadness of the people around me were seeping into my own heart.

2. How did you discover the Seven Laws of Noah?

It all began when my mother-in-law's sister, a deeply pious woman with a strong love for Israel, started sharing Jewish booklets and magazines with me, including *Jewish Actual News*. I had never encountered Jewish perspectives firsthand before, and I found them intriguing. The Jewish worldview seemed rooted in something ancient and structured, yet I had always assumed that, as a Christian, I already possessed the "full" truth.

At first, I viewed Judaism as a small pond compared to the vast ocean of Christianity. After all, Christians had both the Old and New Testaments, surely that meant they had more wisdom. But as I continued exploring, I realized that this so-called "small pond" was filled with profound knowledge. I found a rabbi who welcomed anyone interested in learning, offering teachings from his own home. Eager to deepen my understanding of Torah and seeking solutions to my family's struggles, I began attending his lessons. It was from him that I first heard the mind-blowing idea that the "satan"[7] is rooted in the ego. I had never encountered this concept before! It took time for me to fully grasp, but eventually, I came to understand that this rabbi had saved my marriage. I had been unconsciously repeating the damaging patterns of past generations, and his wisdom helped me break free. His teachings transformed my life completely. Sadly, after some time, he became seriously ill and passed away, leaving me without a guide. Though I felt lost, the questions he had sparked in me remained, urging me to continue my search.

That search led me to Rabbi Dr. Abraham Twerski, a renowned Hassidic Jewish psychiatrist. My sister sent me a short video, called *Fish Love*, in which he explained the idea that true love is about giving, not just taking. He pointed out that the Hebrew word for love, *ahava,* comes from the root meaning "to give." That insight fascinated me, opening the door to even more Jewish wisdom. Before long, I discovered the teachings of Dr. Dovid Lieberman, a psychiatrist whose lectures on personal development, human relationships, and the connection between spirituality and character refinement were available on TorahAnytime.com. As I began listening to his classes, a whole new world unfolded before me.

At first, the terminology was foreign. Many Hebrew words were unfamiliar, and I struggled to grasp the depth of the teachings. Without a teacher to guide me, it took ten years to find my way through Jewish learning.

As my interest in Jewish wisdom deepened, my in-laws began to notice. The warmth with which my mother-in-law's sister had once shared Jewish materials suddenly cooled. The pro-Israel conversations stopped. The booklets and magazines disappeared. I realized that as long as I kept Judaism at a distance, viewing it as

---

7. Referring here to the temptation a person feels to sin.

an interesting culture or historical curiosity, it was acceptable. But the moment I engaged with it seriously, it became a problem.

That, too, was a lesson.

My path to the Seven Laws of Noah was a long, personal journey, a process of peeling back layers, unlearning old assumptions, and allowing myself to step into a truth I had never known existed.

3. What impact did this knowledge have on you?

Let's just say that it changed everything. The Jewish way of explaining the Hebrew Bible had a profound healing effect on me, mentally, emotionally, and even physically. It lifted me up. I began to function better in my marriage, as a mother, and in life as a whole. Learning Torah gave me tools to navigate real-life challenges with a clear mind and with strength.

I discovered that the Torah's understanding of the soul was so much deeper than anything I had encountered before. When the Torah speaks about the soul, it isn't a vague or singular concept; there are five different Hebrew words for it, each representing a different spiritual level. For centuries, the church had systematically burned all Jewish keys to the deeper layers of Torah, leaving generations without access to this wisdom. But as I delved into these teachings, I realized they contained a blueprint for personal growth, inner peace, and emotional resilience.

As I continued studying, something changed within me. The weight I had carried for so long, the sense of smallness, the feeling of being lost, began to fall away. My physical health improved. The stress and anxiety that had once seemed insurmountable became manageable. For the first time in my life, I felt truly equipped to understand and work through the challenges I faced. The more I learned, the stronger and more whole I became.

4. What has been your biggest challenge?

One of my greatest challenges was breaking free from my lack of self-esteem and the exhausting effort of maintaining a façade, hiding my true feelings behind masks of perfectionism. The teachings of Dr. Dovid Lieberman and Rabbi Aryeh Nivin were profoundly healing, helping me uncover my true self beneath the layers of ego that had blocked my soul from connecting to G-d.

I finally understood that true self-esteem is never found within the confines of our comfort zones or through an ego-driven life. Instead, it comes from doing what is right and responsible, regardless of what feels good or appears impressive. I realized that the ego distorts our perception of reality. Once I set my ego aside, I began to see the world as it truly is. For the first time, I recognized the signs that Hashem had been placing along my path all along, things I had been blind to for years. After so much spiritual darkness, these teachers provided me with exactly the lens I needed to finally understand my life's purpose and mission.

The most difficult part of my journey was taking full responsibility for my own spiritual path. I had always followed others, seeking approval. Breaking free, choosing my own way, was painful, but necessary.

5. How has following this path changed your life?

Everything changed for me when I realized that faith is not about suppressing questions, silencing doubts, or endlessly repeating church slogans to reassure myself. It's not about masking pain and insecurities behind a façade of devotion or playing a role to convince myself and others that everything is fine. True faith, I discovered, is about honest self-examination, the willingness to change and grow, and personal responsibility.

For years, I believed that religious devotion meant waiting for a savior to come and solve my problems, because, in the end, that is what Christianity teaches. But as I studied Torah through a Jewish lens, I saw that real faith is about active engagement with wisdom, changing my perspective and behavior, and refusing to passively accept suffering as mere fate. It is not about resigning oneself to "carrying the cross" of misfortune, waiting idly for circumstances to improve, or expecting miracles from an unresponsive idol.

One of the most profound shifts in my thinking was how I viewed suffering. Before, I saw hardship as evidence that others were on the wrong path and that I was merely bearing the burden of their poor choices. But Jewish wisdom taught me to flip the perspective. Suffering is not meaningless, it is a signal, an opportunity to grow, reflect, and find new paths toward positive change. This mindset profoundly transformed how I approached challenges in my marriage, parenting, and personal development.

I also became more intentional about how I lived. The structured cycle of learning the weekly Torah portion *(Parashat HaShavua)* helped me establish a spiritual rhythm filled with meaning. Concepts like *bitachon* and *hishtadlus*[8] reshaped my approach to uncertainty. Instead of feeling powerless, I learned that I had an active role to play in my own life. Trusting Hashem didn't mean doing nothing, it meant making wise, informed choices while knowing that Divine guidance was always present. Jewish teachings empowered me to move forward, leaving behind the limiting beliefs, burdens, and narrow constraints of my personal *Mitzrayim*[9].

---

8. An expression in Hebrew which refers to making a personal effort toward achieving a goal, while also anticipating G-d's help.
9. The Hebrew word for "Egypt". It comes from the word that means "limitations" and "constraints," recalling the enslavement of the Israelites in ancient Egypt.

6. What are you currently learning?

I am studying Jewish wisdom intensely, and my learning continues to evolve. I am part of multiple study groups in both French and Flemish, where we analyze Torah, Jewish mystical texts, ethics, and history. These discussions are not just about accumulating knowledge; they push me to rethink assumptions and apply wisdom to real-life situations.

One of my biggest areas of focus has been Biblical Hebrew. Studying the Torah in its original language has been transformative. I've discovered that Hebrew words hold layers of meaning, mostly lost in translation. For example, *emuna* is commonly translated as "faith," but in Hebrew, it implies something active, faith built through action, discipline, and commitment.

Beyond language, I am also deeply engaged in studying *mussar*, the Jewish discipline of character refinement. Unlike the self-help approaches I had encountered before, *mussar* doesn't just offer abstract ideas about being a better person. It provides structured guidance on overcoming negative traits, developing humility, and practicing gratitude in everyday life. When I discovered the kabbalistic connection of forty-nine levels of human emotion with the Jewish commandment of counting the Omer, I was profoundly moved. This knowledge is a powerful spiritual toolkit to refine one's character traits. I really wonder how differently things might have unfolded had my family discovered this wisdom earlier.

Additionally, I am exploring Jewish perspectives on psychology, self-improvement, and emotional intelligence. The writings of Dr. Dovid Lieberman, and Rabbi Dr. Abraham Twerski have given me profound insights into human nature, how to build resilience, and how to navigate relationships with wisdom and sensitivity.

7. How do you apply what you learn to your daily life?

Applying Jewish wisdom changes you. One of the biggest shifts I see in myself is in how I relate to other people. I understand now that real connection does not come from appearances. It comes from being genuine.I have become more conscious of how I listen, respond, and support others. Instead of surface-level conversations, I strive to engage in deeper, more meaningful interactions. I've also learned to balance kindness with honesty, speaking truth with sensitivity rather than avoidance.

Honoring the seventh day[10] has become a pillar of my life. I prepare my home beautifully, cook a special meal, and set aside time for learning and reflection. For me, this day is a time to step out of the distractions of the world and reconnect with what truly matters. The structure it provides has brought peace, joy, and a deep sense of spiritual renewal to my household.

Additionally, I am more mindful of my speech, aware of the power of words to uplift or harm. I practice *hakarat hatov* (being appreciative for the good), shifting my focus from what is lacking to what I have. This shift in perspective has brought more gratitude and contentment into my life.

Another major transformation is how I handle uncertainty. I used to struggle with anxiety, constantly fearing the unknown. But through Jewish wisdom, I have learned to cultivate *bitachon*, trust in Hashem's plan. This doesn't mean passively waiting for things to improve, but rather taking thoughtful action while knowing that not everything is within my control. This balance of effort and trust has helped me navigate challenges with a greater sense of calm and purpose.

---

10. In ways appropriate for Noahides; see Additional Information, pg. 199).

My home feels different, my interactions feel different, and most importantly, I feel different. This knowledge has not only changed how I see the world, but how I move through it. And I believe there are many people out there who could benefit from it, if only they were willing to open their eyes.

KEY LESSONS

1. **True wisdom is found in the layers of Torah, not in a sentimental "additional testament."** I once thought the New Testament's emotional approach brought transformation, but Torah contains profound and lasting meaning. Discovering its Hebrew words for the five soul-levels revealed how much had been disregarded. Now I study with a teacher fluent in Biblical Hebrew, learning that true wisdom unfolds over a lifetime.

2. **Authenticity, not forced appearances, creates true connection.** For years, I was surrounded by people who avoided deep conversations and focused on appearances. Now, I know real connection comes from honesty. I engage in meaningful conversations, listen more, and seek relationships built on truth rather than social performance.

3. **Healing comes through knowledge, not by "becoming like a child" as church teachings suggested.** I've seen the damage caused by emotional immaturity. I once believed a savior would fix everything, but Torah showed me that healing comes from understanding of self, relationships, and growth. Jewish wisdom has uplifted me spiritually and improved my well-being and relationships.

4. **Struggles are invitations to seek deeper truth, not signs of failure.** I once saw hardship as proof that a "devil" had power over me, but struggles are not meant to disempower. Instead, they can teach. Every challenge, from childhood pain to questioning faith, led me to deeper truth. Now, I ask, "What can I learn from this?" instead of "Why is this happening to me?"

5. **Love is about giving, not just receiving.** Rabbi Twerski's insight about "fish love" reshaped my relationships. Love isn't about taking, it's about giving. The Hebrew word for love, *ahava*, comes from the word "to give." I now focus on contributing, making my relationships deeper and more fulfilling.

6. **Honoring wisdom, questioning deeply, and honoring the seventh day brings peace.** My search for truth once felt unstable, but now I have structure. The seventh day is a source of peace. Preparing my home, cooking, and setting aside time for study brings stability. It brings more than a reset; it's a time to reconnect with what matters.

7. **Challenging knowledge is a tool for growth, not something to fear.** At first, questioning felt like betrayal. But truth withstands scrutiny. Instead of fearing new knowledge, I welcome difficult questions, knowing they lead to greater understanding. Growth comes from challenging old beliefs and expanding perspectives.

2.

Daniel ben Noah | (United Kingdom)

MEANING IN EVERY STEP: A NOAHIDE'S WAY

"What began as a niggling discomfort with church doctrine slowly unfolded into a journey of searching, questioning, and ultimately embracing the Torah's truth, a path that gave my life the clarity and meaning I'd long been seeking."

1. What is your background?

I was raised in a Christian family with Orthodox roots. Our home life was often difficult, marked by emotional distance, instability, and miscommunication. My father struggled with alcohol and spent much of my childhood working abroad. When he was home, emotional connection was hard to find. My mother, of blessed memory, carried the weight of raising my younger brother and me largely on her own. While I now understand how much she was trying to hold everything together, our relationship was strained during those years.

We observed Christian holidays like Easter and New Year, but religion felt more cultural than personal. Occasionally, my mother would send me to church to light candles before icons and images. I followed her instructions, but something never sat right with me. That inner conflict sharpened when, around age fifteen, I read the Second Commandment: not to make or worship graven images. Yet the church was full of them. I didn't bring it up, but that moment did change something in me. It was then that I began to distance myself from Christian practices.

At nearly eighteen, I moved to Spain to live with my father. I hoped it might help us rebuild our connection, but it was an emotionally difficult time. Still, it gave me space to think. A few years later, I moved to the UK to improve my English and start fresh. During those transitions, something in me kept searching.

2. How did you discover the Seven Laws of Noah?

While in Spain, I made friends who brought me to Protestant churches. I went with an open mind and curiosity, but couldn't understand the overwhelming focus on Jesus and the New Testament. Why was there so little attention on the Old Testament, which had always felt more genuine to me? Other churches I visited were even more emotionally intense, with group singing, raised hands, and declarations of being "saved." None of it resonated. I eventually stepped away from church entirely and didn't identify with any religious practice for nearly eight years.

In my late twenties, I went through a period of personal struggle. With hope, I began to pray to G-d, not with formal words, but in the only way I knew how. I spoke honestly, admitting to mistakes I had been trying to bury in my mind for years. I also asked for truth and guidance. That sincere prayer sparked a change. I began exploring world religions. I considered reading the Quran, glanced at Hinduism and Buddhism, but none of them resonated. Then one day I asked myself a simple question: what do the Jewish people believe?

That question led me to discover the Torah, the *Tanach*[11], and eventually to the teachings of Rabbi Tovia Singer. His YouTube videos helped me understand what Judaism actually teaches. Because his explanations were grounded in scripture, I began, for the first time, to clearly see the contradictions in the New Testament. Rabbi Singer's deep respect for sources and his patient explanations felt like a lifeline. That's when I learned about the Seven Laws of Noah, not as a new faith, but as an ancient truth for non-Jews who want to live righteously.

3. What impact did this knowledge have on you?

Torah brought a new steadiness into my life. It helped me make sense of things, quieted my thoughts. I began studying with intensity, buying books, watching classes, and trying to absorb everything I could.

At first, I was excited to share what I was learning with family and friends. I thought they would be just as amazed. But most weren't receptive. That disappointment helped me refocus inward. Instead of trying to change others, I committed to changing myself, my character, my thinking, and my actions. My goal became to live what I had found, not just speak about it.

4. What has been your biggest challenge?

Walking this path without a local Noahide community has been one of the hardest challenges. It can feel isolating when you don't have people around who share your values or spiritual worldview. But Hashem provided help through online classes, virtual communities, and wise teachers I've encountered from afar.

---

11. The complete 24 Books of the Hebrew Bible. See fn. 3.

Another challenge has been unlearning the belief that spirituality means giving everything up. I used to think that in order to be righteous, I had to sacrifice all stability. But the Torah taught me something different, that having steady work, healthy relationships, and a meaningful daily routine is not only good, it's essential. These aren't distractions from spiritual life, they're the foundation of it.

5. How has following this path changed your life?

It has changed how I think, how I act, and how I see the world. I have become more thoughtful, more honest with myself, and more aware of how much inner work still lies ahead. I do not see challenges the way I used to. I no longer assume they mean I am doing something wrong. Often, they are exactly the places where I am being forced to grow.

I have also come to trust Hashem more deeply, though not in a constant or perfect way. Sometimes I feel guided and grounded, and sometimes I feel confused, emotional, or unsure. I do not move through life with steady clarity all the time. But I keep returning to the sense that I am trying to walk in truth, and that affects the choices I make, the way I respond, and the way I try to live.

6. What are you currently learning?

I'm part of the Sukkat Shalom–B'nei Noah online community, where we have classes with Rabbi Tani Burton, Rabbi Tuvia Serber, and occasional guest speakers. I'm studying *The Seven Gates of Righteous Knowledge* by Rabbi Moshe Weiner and Dr. Michael Schulman. This book has been a powerful tool in helping me understand the Noahide worldview in a structured, grounded way.

I also study the weekly Torah portion from the *Chumash*[12], with attention to the traditional Jewish commentaries. I'm especially drawn to the stories of the kings of Israel. Their journeys, marked by mistakes, repentance, humility, and responsibility, mirror many of the lessons I've needed to learn in my own life. I also study *middot*[13], like patience, gratitude, and humility—not just in theory, but as practical tools to refine how I live.

7. How do you apply what you learn to your daily life?

I try to begin and end my day with prayer and gratitude. I spend a few minutes a day speaking to Hashem in my own words and study a little Torah each day, even if it's brief. I reflect on what I learn and how it applies to my daily decisions.

I try to bring awareness into each moment. The way I treat others, the way I respond to stress, the words I use, all of that is part of serving Hashem.

I also carry the hope of building a home with a woman who shares this path. I believe that the partner we choose is one of the most important decisions in life. I pray to find someone who values Torah, kindness, and spiritual growth, so that we can walk this journey together.

---

12. The name in Hebrew for The Five Books of Moses.
13. The word in Hebrew for traits of character.

KEY LESSONS

1. **Truth is available, but it must be searched for with sincerity.** I didn't find truth by following crowds or trends, but by following questions that refused to go away. A sincere heart can pierce through confusion.

2. **Prayer, even simple and personal, can open unexpected doors.** When I began praying in my own words, confessing mistakes I had tried for years to push out of my memory, it changed the course of my life. It wasn't formal or scripted. It was real, sincere, and Hashem responded.

3. **Torah wisdom isn't just knowledge, it's a blueprint for life.** The Torah isn't abstract philosophy. It's practical guidance that touches every part of how we live, think, speak, and treat others.

4. **Stability isn't the opposite of spirituality; it's what allows it to flourish.** I used to think striving for holiness meant hardship, but I've learned that a steady job, a peaceful home, and daily rhythm are what support a Torah-centered life.

5. **You don't need to convert to live a life of meaning and service.** The Seven Laws of Noah are a dignified, sacred path. I didn't have to become someone else, I just had to live as myself, with purpose and commitment.

6. **Spiritual growth means refining your character, one day at a time.** Patience, humility, gratitude; these aren't traits you master overnight. But the work of refining them is the real spiritual path.

7. **Walking this path may be lonely, but Hashem never leaves you alone.** Even without a local community, I've found connection, support, and Divine guidance in unexpected places. Every sincere step is accompanied from above.

3.

Boaz ben Noah | (Netherlands)

A PATH OF FAITH, IDENTITY, AND UNDERSTANDING

"Seeking truth requires rigorous questioning; accepting easy answers was never an option."

1. What is your background?

I grew up in a Christian household. I was generally raised in an Evangelical environment. My parents were divorced, and my mother passed away when I was about sixteen years old. Around that time, I had no contact with my father.

During my teenage years, my mother was quite religiously searching. We frequently moved from one church to another. Looking back, I realize that I have no problem standing alone because my mother was always somewhat of an outsider. She did that to herself, but it also shaped my perspective.

At a certain point, I was quite pro-Israel and influenced by many aspects of Evangelical Christianity. However, when my first relationship ended, I found myself reassessing and reevaluating many things in life. In the early 2000's, I had already stopped attending church. I couldn't fit it into my work schedule, which made it difficult. However, I did try to attend some midweek small group meetings.

I became increasingly aware of my search for meaning, values, and the things I wanted to hold onto and redefine. Around 2016 I met Judith. We both had similar questions and had left certain things behind, recognizing that we hadn't always made the right choices. We wanted a fresh start.

2. How did you discover the Seven Laws of Noah?

At a friend's birthday party, I had a conversation with someone that changed my perspective. I had many questions, mainly about the teachings of the apostle Paul. He made all these declarations, but I always wondered, why was *he* the one to determine these things? If Jesus said something in the New Testament, that held value for me at the time, but Paul's authority was a question mark for me.

That led me to a discussion where someone suggested attending a Jewish study house in Rotterdam, where I could ask questions and receive answers. Judith and I decided to check it out and she was the one who suggested looking for discussions between a rabbi and a Christian pastor.

That's when I encountered Rabbi Tovia Singer. It was a turning point. He articulated the beliefs I already held but provided answers no one else could. It was as if I fell into a void; I hadn't seen this coming. That realization led me to reach out to my Christian community to discuss my research and doubts. However, the response I received was often, "I believe in Jesus because he means so much to me personally." But I wasn't looking for personal experiences; I was seeking answers.

3. What impact did this knowledge have on you?

I realized that Christian beliefs often rely heavily on emotional persuasion rather than knowledge-based arguments. That quickly led me to a dead-end, and I knew I needed to pursue something different. Judith and I walked this path together, discussing these deep issues with with her father, who was also a Christian. Our conversations were intense but always respectful. Eventually, he made the same transition we did. He was the one who actively sought out a Jewish community for us to join.

At first, we tried the Rotterdam community, but for various reasons, we left. Then Judith's father found a community in Utrecht. He took the initiative to reach out, and it turned out we were very welcome. Through that connection, we eventually found our way into studying Judaism more in-depth, and we joined the Dutch Noahide Community.

4. What has been your biggest challenge?

One of the biggest challenges I faced was adjusting my language and manner of speaking. Coming from South Holland, my language was often rough, and I struggled with choosing my words carefully. That remains an area where I am consciously improving.

Regarding relationships, my family accepted my choice completely. My father, for example, wore a *kippah*[14] at my wedding without issue. Judith's side had more discussions, especially with her grandfather, who was more traditional in his Christian beliefs.

Most of my friends remained Christian, but we maintained mutual respect. Some were curious and asked questions about my transition. Occasionally, I engage in discussions with Christians who challenge my beliefs, but I enjoy those conversations as long as they remain respectful.

14. The word in Hebrew for a Jewish-style skullcap (yarmulke).

5. How has following this path changed your life?

My life changed significantly due to this path, especially because it led me to meet my wife. We initially connected through a Christian dating site, but we both already had many questions about our faith. Our transition toward Judaism was a joint journey, where we constantly challenged and reassessed our beliefs.

During that time, I also left my work in the theater industry because I increasingly felt discomfort with religious themes and elements in certain performances. I moved away from the artistic side and into the technical side of the industry to avoid exposure to conflicting ideologies.

6. What are you currently learning?

In my current studies, I follow several rabbis, including Rabbi Tovia Singer, Rabbi Skobac, and Rabbi Keleman. Each has provided valuable perspectives. I find the study of Jewish law and the Oral Tradition particularly fascinating. It was eye-opening to realize that many Christian teachings misrepresented Jewish texts.

7. How do you apply what you learn to your daily life?

Applying what I've learned to daily life is an ongoing process. We incorporate morning prayers into our routine and have structured learning sessions. However, I am also cautious about adopting practices that are specific to Jews. I want to be respectful of boundaries while integrating the values and teachings into my life.

A significant shift in my mindset has been learning to accept difficult situations with the understanding that they serve a higher purpose, even if I don't fully comprehend it. This has helped me deal with challenges in a more composed manner.

Choosing my Hebrew name, Boaz, was also a deliberate step in marking this transition. My birth name was Christiaan

Stefanus, but I no longer felt comfortable with a name that tied me to Christian martyrdom. I wanted a name that reflected my journey. I chose Boaz because of the Biblical connection, while Ruth was the one who entered Judaism from outside, Boaz played a crucial role in integrating her into the Jewish people.

Overall, this journey has deepened my search for truth and given me a framework for engaging in intellectual discussions about faith. I am open to debates, and I enjoy challenging and being challenged by different perspectives. My experience has reinforced my belief that seeking truth requires rigorous questioning, and I continue to learn and refine my understanding every day.

KEY LESSONS

1. **Questioning is the first step to growth.** My journey started the moment I allowed myself to question. I always struggled with Paul's authority; why was he the one to determine the doctrine? That led me to search beyond Christianity. Real growth happens when we stop accepting things at face value and start digging deeper.

2. **Emotional beliefs can't replace rational inquiry.** When I voiced my doubts, the response was often, "I believe in Jesus because he means so much to me personally." But I wasn't looking for personal feelings, I wanted solid answers. The more I examined Christian teachings, the more I saw how much they relied on emotion rather than knowledge. This pushed me further toward Judaism, where study and reason take precedence.

3. **Transitions require courage.** Walking away from Christianity wasn't easy. It also affected my work; I became uncomfortable with religious themes in theater and shifted to the technical side to avoid conflicts with my beliefs. Every transition required courage.

4. **Community matters, but truth comes first.** Finding the right community played a role in my transition, but truth always came first. Judith and I walked this path together, but we needed support beyond each other. Her father, once a devout Christian, helped us find a Jewish community in Utrecht. Community is vital, but it can't be the reason for faith.

5. **Respectful dialogue opens doors.** Not everyone in my life agreed with my choices, but I always approached conversations with respect. Most of my friends remained Christian, but we maintained mutual understanding. I enjoy discussing theology, even when challenged, as long as it fosters deeper thought rather than conflict.

6. **Identity is an ongoing journey.** Changing my name to Boaz was a symbolic step. My birth name no longer reflected who I was. I chose Boaz because, in the Biblical story, he played a key role in welcoming Ruth into Judaism.

7. **Challenges have purpose.** Adjusting hasn't always been easy. One of my biggest challenges was changing the way I spoke. Coming from South Holland, my language was often rough, and I had to learn to be more intentional with my words. But I've learned to see challenges differently, not as obstacles, but as opportunities for growth.

4.

Judith bat Noah | (Netherlands)

BREAKING CHAINS, A NOAHIDE AWAKENING

"Everything comes from Hashem, even the challenges. My job is not to resist, but to ask, 'What can I learn from this?' "

1. What is your background?

I was raised in a Christian household, growing up in a Pentecostal church where I was very active. My family had a more Reformed, Calvinistic background. My parents both became "born again" during their early twenties and joined a Pentecostal congregation, which is where I grew up. I also attended a Reformed school, creating an interesting dynamic in my upbringing.

At home, discussions about the Bible and theology were frequent, and we were encouraged to study the scriptures. I was very involved in church life and even joined an evangelism group as a teenager. This was something I felt deeply connected to and pursued with passion.

I always had a strong interest in theology, particularly in eschatology (end times). My family nurtured this curiosity, and I read extensively on the subject, as well as on replacement theology and the role of Israel. My parents took me to events organized by Christians for Israel, and I even sang in a children's choir that performed at those gatherings.

When I was about ten years old, I had to do a school project, and while my classmates chose topics like horses or hospitals, I chose kosher food. I was already fascinated by it. At fifteen, I had the opportunity to take Hebrew as an elective in school. I was already learning Greek at the time, so I was deeply engaged with scriptural texts. The ability to read the Hebrew Bible in its authentic language was something I found incredibly meaningful.

2. How did you discover the Seven Laws of Noah?

At nineteen, I married my first husband, a charismatic but deeply troubled man. He suffered from severe mental health challenges, including manic depression. Our relationship was unpredictable, he was always searching, always restless. We tried different churches, but he struggled to fit in. Conflicts and provocations often led to our departure from congregations, and over time, I found myself becoming detached from church life.

When he passed away, my life was turned upside down. I moved in with my father for over a year to rebuild my life. During that time, I tried returning to my childhood congregation, where my mother was still very much involved. At first, it felt familiar and comforting, but I soon realized I no longer belonged. I had too many unanswered questions, and the teachings no longer fit what I had come to understand.

My father played a crucial role in my discovery of the Seven Laws of Noah. He had always encouraged discussions and critical thinking. He was pragmatic, when confronted with a question, he sought direct answers. As I was searching, he joined me in exploring alternative perspectives.

During this time I met Boaz, and we found out we shared a lot of the same questions concerning Christianity. We came across a group in Rotterdam that hosted Jewish learning sessions, where non-Jews were welcome to study and ask questions. That was where I first encountered the Seven Laws of Noah.

3. What impact did this knowledge have on you?

Learning about the Seven Laws of Noah opened up a whole new path. Boaz and I started watching lectures by rabbis, reading Jewish texts, and joining study groups. It was exciting, but also unsettling at times. I had been raised to view the entire Christian Bible as G-d's word and to search for Jesus in every passage. Now I found myself rethinking it all.

One of the most powerful moments was encountering *Isaiah 45:7*, "I form the light and create darkness; I make peace and create evil; I, Hashem, do all these things." This completely contradicted the Christian belief that evil comes from an adversary of G-d. If G-d is truly One, then there can be no duality; He must be the source of all things.

Another defining moment was reading *Ezekiel 18*, which clearly states that no one can die for another person's sins. That shook me to my core. If the Torah is true, then the foundational Christian doctrine of atonement through Jesus could not be. Accepting that realization took time, but once I did, there was no turning back.

4. What has been your biggest challenge?

One of my greatest challenges has been internalizing the awareness of Divine unity in daily life, especially when it comes to emotions like anger. When I feel angry, I remind myself that everything comes from Hashem and that everything has a purpose. Instead of resisting, I try to ask, "What am I supposed to learn from this?"

Music has also been difficult. I grew up immersed in Christian music, Keith Green, Elly and Rikkert, and the Opwekking worship songs. Music from your youth is deeply connected to emotions and memories, and it was hard to let go of something that had been such a big part of my life. Many of the lyrics now feel like idolatry to me, so I have consciously distanced myself from them. Instead, I listen to Jewish music, but detaching from those emotional connections has been an ongoing process.

5. How has following this path changed your life?

Leaving Christianity was not an emotional decision, it was a decision based on truth. I had to acknowledge that what I once believed no longer held up under scrutiny. Yet, despite having a wonderful childhood and family memories associated with Christianity, I knew I had to follow the path that aligned with reality.

I also see parallels between leaving Christianity and the end of my first marriage. My husband had convinced me that I needed him, that I couldn't do certain things on my own. After he was gone, I realized I was capable. In the same way, Christianity had conditioned me to believe that I needed an intermediary to reach G-d. Once I stepped away, I realized that I didn't. I could turn directly to Hashem.

My connection to Torah and Hashem has given me more stability and a clearer way forward.

6. What are you currently learning?

I follow the weekly Torah portion and study *Tanya*[15] daily, which is incredibly complex. Sometimes, after listening to a half-hour explanation, I still feel like I understand nothing. But over time, I absorb more and more. I also listen to lectures by rabbis like Rabbi

---

15. Title of a foundational work of Hassidic teachings by the first Chabad Rebbe, Rabbi Shneur Zalman. See Additional Information, pg. 199.

Breitowitz and Rabbi Richman, and to Rabanit K. Sarah Cohen, particularly on Jewish thought and ethics.

7. How do you apply what you learn to your daily life?

I strive to avoid anger, to see situations positively, and to speak well of others. I practice *tzniut*[16], not just in clothing, but I try to apply this also in behavior, along with listening more and speaking with intention.

I cover my hair as a way of symbolizing the sanctity of marriage[17]. It also helps me establish personal boundaries, given my past experiences. In the beginning, it felt strange, but now it feels completely natural.

My mother found it difficult at first, but my father accepted it. My grandmother, who has dementia, didn't fully understand; she would say, "I like your scarf, but now take it off." But ultimately, my family respects my decision.

I believe more people are discovering the Noahide path. And within the Jewish community, I see growing awareness and acceptance. The Lubavitcher Rebbe actively encouraged the spread of Noahide teachings[18], and we see in prophecy that knowledge of Hashem will one day spread across the world like water covering the seabed[19]. I believe we are witnessing that unfold in our time.

---

16. The word in Hebrew for "modesty", in dressing and behavior.
17. The Talmud relates that there were societies where this was practiced to some extent by non-Jewish married woman, and some rabbis encourage the continuation of this practice. There are details within Torah law of how this is to be observed by Jewish married women.
18. See *To Perfect the World: The Lubavitcher Rebbe's Call to Teach the Noahide Code to All Mankind*, 2nd Edition, pub. Sichos In English.
19. From Isaiah 11:9.

KEY LESSONS

1. **Truth matters more than comfort, even when it is painful.** I did not leave Christianity because I was unhappy. I left because I found contradictions I could no longer ignore, and I knew that staying with something I no longer believed would not bring me closer to Hashem.

2. **Faith is a journey, not a destination, and growth requires questioning.** I once thought I had all the answers, but discovering the Noahide path showed me that real wisdom comes from asking better questions and never being afraid of where the truth might lead.

3. **Hashem is One, and that changed the way I see the world.** Understanding His unity resolved many of the contradictions I had wrestled with for years. It gave me a clearer way of looking at life, with the understanding that nothing is separate from Him and that nothing happens without purpose.

4. **The heart does not always move as quickly as the mind.** I had to let go of what felt familiar and safe in order to follow what I had come to see as true. That was not easy. But I trusted that, in time, peace would come with living in alignment with the truth.

5. **I am responsible for my own choices, and no one else can carry that for me.** No one can atone for me, and no one can dictate my relationship with Hashem. I have the power and the responsibility to shape my own spiritual path.

6. **Challenges are not punishments; they are lessons designed to refine me.** Even my struggles—being in a challenging marriage, and then losing my first husband, leaving my former faith, and starting over—became stepping stones to a deeper understanding of Hashem and a stronger sense of who I truly am.

7. **Modesty is about more than clothing; it's about presence, dignity, and self-respect.** Covering my hair is a personal commitment, but true modesty also means refining my speech, my actions, my thoughts, and how I present myself to the world, focusing on inner substance over external appearance.

5.

Fumani Brian Hlekani | (South Africa)

MY JOURNEY TO GROWTH AND PURPOSE

"When I shifted my focus to gratitude, life's challenges became lessons, and I finally understood that everything, good or bad, is part of Hashem's plan for me."

1. What is your background?

My name is Fumani Brian Hlekani. I was born on July 9, 1981, in Kian, a small village in Limpopo, South Africa. Life in the village was simple, and tough. My mom raised my younger sister and me, while my five half-brothers lived with my father. Unfortunately, my father passed away before I ever met him.

We were a close-knit community. I grew up attending a church called Swiss Mission, started by missionaries in our village. When I was fifteen, I moved to Johannesburg, a big change from the quiet life I knew. I finished school there and started working for myself.

I've always been entrepreneurial. I ran my own IT business and later moved into human resources consulting. But even with these accomplishments, I felt like something was missing in my life, like I was searching for a deeper meaning.

2. How did you discover the Seven Laws of Noah?

It all started when my cousin invited me to a conference where Rabbi Brody was speaking. I didn't know much about him or what the conference was about, but I went, and it changed my life.

Rabbi Brody spoke about the Seven Noahide Laws, and it felt like his message was meant for me. I left the event feeling both peaceful and curious. I knew I had found something important, even if I didn't fully understand it yet.

From there, I started learning more. I listened to Rabbi Brody's online classes and discovered TorahAnytime.com, a website with daily lessons. Those lessons gave me direction and helped me see how the Seven Laws could guide my life.

3. What impact did this knowledge have on you?

Before I learned about the Seven Laws, I was always questioning things, like, why wasn't I married? Why did certain struggles keep happening? Studying the Seven Lawshas given me a new perspective. I began to see that everything happens for a reason and that there's a bigger plan.

One of the biggest changes was learning to focus on gratitude. Instead of worrying about what I didn't have, I started appreciating what I do have. That shift brought a lot of peace to my life. My family noticed the change, too; they often comment on how calm and grounded I've become.

There have been challenges, like when my car was broken into and I lost my laptop, personal items, and a journal full of Torah notes. I was devastated, but I reminded myself of something Rabbi Brody teaches: challenges are opportunities to grow. That mindset helped me move forward and still does.

4. What has been your biggest challenge?

One of the hardest things has been balancing my beliefs with what my friends and family believe. Not everyone in my life understands or agrees with what I've learned, and I've had to learn how to handle those differences carefully.

Another challenge has been finding a community. A Jewish neighbor once invited me to synagogue, but I was hesitant. I worried about not fitting in. It's something I'm still working on, to have the confidence to connect with others who share these values.

5. How has following this path changed your life?

Learning about the Seven Noahide Laws has brought stability and purpose to my life. I'm more patient and grateful, and I've learned to handle challenges with a better attitude.

It's also changed how I think about my future. I hope to get married one day, but now I understand it's about more than just finding a partner. It's about building a life with shared values and purpose.

6. What are you currently learning?

Right now, I'm focused on understanding the practical and ethical aspects of the Seven Laws. It amazes me how these teachings, written so long ago, are still relevant today.

I study for about an hour every day, often using TorahAnytime.com or Rabbi Brody's lessons. Each day, I learn something new that helps me better understand how to live by these principles.

7. How do you apply what you learn to your daily life?

I try to apply what I learn in small, consistent ways. Gratitude is a big part of it. When I feel stressed or frustrated, I take a moment to thank Hashem for the good things in my life.

At work, these lessons help me stay calm and patient, even in tough situations. I approach my HR consulting work with a focus on deep listening, which has improved my relationships overall.

Most of all, I try to live in a way that shows how these teachings have helped me. It's not just about what I believe; it's about how I live my life.

KEY LESSONS

1. **Gratitude changes everything.** When I started focusing on what I have instead of what I lack, my entire outlook on life changed. Gratitude brought me peace, stability, and a deeper appreciation for life's blessings.

2. **Challenges are here to teach us.** Even when my laptop, journal and other belongings were stolen, I realized that hardships can help us grow stronger and more resilient. Every challenge is an opportunity to learn and improve.

3. **There's a reason for everything.** Accepting that life's ups and downs are part of a bigger plan has given me peace and clarity. Trusting that Hashem's plan is always for the best has changed how I respond to difficulties.

4. **Relationships require patience and understanding.** Navigating differences in belief with loved ones has shown me how important balance and respect are. Faith is personal, but relationships thrive when we approach them with kindness and patience.

5. **Values give life meaning.** I've learned that building a meaningful future is about living by principles, not just achieving goals. The Seven Noahide Laws have given me a moral and ethical framework to guide my life.

6. **Knowledge transforms perspective.** Learning about the Seven Noahide Laws reshaped my mindset, helping me see the world through a lens of purpose and responsibility. Understanding these teachings has made me a better person.

7. **Faith is lived through actions.** Faith isn't just about beliefs; it's about how we live. Applying what I've learned, through gratitude, patience, and ethical decisions, has allowed me to embody the values that guide my journey.

6.

Channah Elanna Hadassah bat Noah | (Netherlands)

THE SEVEN LAWS OF NOAH AS MY LIFE'S PATH

"Living as a Noahide has taught me that G-d's design for humanity is both universal and personal, rooted in timeless values that connect us all while honoring our unique paths."

1. What is your background?

From a young age, I felt an innate and deeply personal connection to G-d. Even as a child, I sensed that my relationship with G-d was uniquely my own. Children's Bible stories felt too simplistic and unsatisfying to me, so I began creating what I called an "adult Bible" for kids. I rewrote stories and paired them with illustrations, not realizing I was crafting an entirely new children's Bible.

Some of my most profound spiritual experiences happened at night. I would slip outside into the garden under the stars to speak with G-d in the stillness. Those moments were filled with awe and intimacy, leaving a deep impression on my soul. To this day, I long for the closeness I felt during those quiet moments.

At age thirteen, I was baptized. It was a significant milestone but not without challenges. The minister initially doubted that I was ready for such a commitment. Still, as tradition dictated, I was baptized in the name of "the Father, the Son, and the Holy Spirit." Even then, my view of Jesus differed from what was traditionally taught. In my confession, I described Jesus as an elder brother and role model rather than G-d incarnate. While he was central to my faith, I did not equate him with G-d.

Shortly after, my parents joined a small Christian group with ultra-dispensationalist beliefs. Our affiliation with this group led to our expulsion from the church. Losing my peer group and spiritual community was devastating. I felt abandoned by those who had pledged to walk alongside me on my journey of faith.

This experience, however, planted the seeds of critical thinking and questioning Christian scripture. I learned that staying true to one's convictions often comes at a cost, but that cost is worth paying for authenticity and faithfulness.

2. How did you discover the Seven Laws of Noah?

My journey toward embracing the Seven Laws of Noah began during my teenage years, at the dawn of the Internet age. I came across an article about Noahides, a concept that piqued my curiosity but which I quickly dismissed when I learned that Noahides did not believe in Jesus. At the time, this felt like a direct affront to everything I had been taught. I labeled it a doctrine of Satan and moved on.

Years later, during one of the most trying periods of my life, this concept resurfaced unexpectedly. My mother became critically ill and had to depend on others for care, something she found deeply difficult because she had always been so fiercely independent. Her physical and emotional suffering made me feel desperate. Despite my prayers and years of devotion, G-d seemed silent. I felt abandoned and began to question the very foundation of what I believed.

Amid this turmoil, my mother reminded me of a promise I had made as a teenager, to assist her with euthanasia if she ever became dependent. The weight of her request was to much. I agonized for months, knowing it would harm both her soul and mine. In the end, I refused. This decision created a rift between us, leaving me with overwhelming anger, rejection from both my parents. and a sense of isolation. The verse of *Psalm 27:10*, "For though my father and my mother have forsaken me, the L-rd has taken me in." That felt like my verse at that moment, with the difference that I also felt abandoned by G-d, but had hope that He would accept me.

A year later, my father shocked me with news that my mother's euthanasia was scheduled for the following week. I was heartbroken but managed to negotiate a chance to say goodbye. Though our farewell was strained, it allowed me to express gratitude for her role as my mother, a moment I will always treasure.

On the day of her passing, my mother expressed a wish for me to be present. The experience was cold and clinical, the most undignified death I could have imagined. She had chosen to donate her body to science, which meant no funeral, no memorial, no closure. The day after, I felt utterly lost, grappling with the enormity of what had happened.

Seeking solace, my husband and I went for a walk in northern Germany, exploring a forest we had never visited. As we strolled, we heard an unusual sound above us. I joked, "Maybe we'll see crane birds again," recalling a comforting moment shortly before her death when I saw two rare cranes. Emerging from the forest, we encountered a field filled with over a thousand cranes, a breathtaking sight I had never seen before or since. In that moment, I felt a profound sense of reassurance, as though G-d was offering me comfort.

As spring arrived, so did Passover, a season that always brought introspection. Every year, I struggled with the idea that "Jesus died for your sins." The concept seemed unjust: why should someone else bear the consequences of my actions? This question haunted me annually, surfacing around Passover and lingering unresolved before fading into the background.

This year, I decided it was time to confront these doubts. I sought answers from both a pastor and a rabbi. The pastor offered little, no written explanations, no personal insights. This silence was disheartening but clarifying. It became clear that I did not belong to a community unable to address my deepest questions.

In contrast, the rabbi's responses were thoughtful and thorough. Through emails and phone calls, he provided answers that resonated deeply, though each answer prompted new questions. I see this rabbi as my spiritual father, as without him I would never have taken the steps I was allowed to take, and his guidance laid the foundation for my growing understanding while encouraging me to critically reexamine my beliefs.

Over the forty days leading up to Passover, I let go of doubts, attachments, and a framework that no longer felt authentic. This was followed by the forty-nine days of the Omer, during which I embraced a new identity and purpose. While I had not yet fully transitioned to Judaism, I found peace in the principles of Noahidism, a universal path that brought clarity and harmony to my spiritual journey.

Guided by Rabbi Tovia Singer's personal teachings, I delved deeper into Judaism and discovered the Seven Laws of Noah through a prayer booklet I found online from Asknoah.org. This framework offered the clarity, truth, and sense of purpose I had been searching for.

This period marked a profound turning point in my life. Every question, every exploration, and every reflection brought me closer to understanding my role in G-d's greater plan. My journey became not just about seeking answers but about transformation, aligning my life with the Divine purpose I had been searching for all along.

3. What impact did this knowledge have on you?

Discovering the Seven Laws of Noah was a transformative revelation. For years, I struggled with the inconsistencies of my Christian upbringing and the contradictions in Messianic beliefs. The Seven Laws provided the clarity and structure I had been searching for. It was as though the fragmented pieces of my spiritual journey finally formed a coherent and beautiful picture.

The universality of the Seven Laws struck me deeply. These principles, grounded in morality, justice, and the sanctity of life, are not bound by culture or historical context. They apply to all humanity, offering a timeless and inclusive framework for righteous living. This universality fostered a profound sense of connection, not just to G-d but to humanity as a whole.

I delved into texts like *The Divine Code* and *Seven Gates of Righteous Knowledge* by Rabbi Moshe Weiner. These resources clarified the distinction between the 613 commandments for Jews and the Seven Laws for non-Jews, emphasizing the focus on universal messages rather than adopting Jewish rituals. Translating Rabbi Weiner's *Bi'ur Torat Moshe*[20] into Dutch felt like the culmination of my spiritual journey, echoing my childhood dream of making Biblical teachings accessible. This work affirmed my purpose: to teach, share, and spread awareness of the Noahide Laws.

The transformative power of these teachings extended to my everyday life. The Seven Laws didn't just provide a spiritual framework; they reshaped how I viewed ethical responsibility. I began to see every action as an opportunity to reflect Divine values. Whether in family interactions, professional decisions, or community involvement, I was motivated to align my behavior with these universal principles.

---

20. A book of explanations for Noahides of the verses Genesis 1:1-6:8.

4. What has been your biggest challenge?

One of my biggest challenges has been accepting G-d's decision not to create me as a Jew. While I feel a deep connection to Judaism and its teachings, I strive to trust in G-d's wisdom and embrace the path He has set for me as a Noahide, even when it doesn't align with my personal desires. Each morning, I pray and thank G-d for creating me according to His will, resolving to serve Him faithfully in the place where He needs me most.

At the same time, I wrestle with questions about my role and purpose. Could being created according to His will also mean that He desires me to take the steps toward becoming Jewish? The Noahide path offers a unique freedom to shape my relationship with G-d in a deeply personal way, but I wonder whether I could ever fulfill the intricate commandments and responsibilities required of a Jewish life. These questions challenge me to reflect on how I can best fulfill my purpose, improve the world, and become the person G-d intends me to be.

Living as a Noahide brings its own challenges. The path is often misunderstood, even within Jewish communities, which can sometimes lead to feelings of isolation. It can be difficult to explain that the Noahide framework is a complete and valid spiritual identity, not necessarily a stepping stone to conversion. Additionally, the lack of structured rituals or institutions means I must take full responsibility for my spiritual growth and remain committed to the Seven Laws on my own initiative.

Despite these struggles, the Noahide path has also brought profound meaning to my life. It allows me to cultivate a deeply personal connection with G-d, one shaped by my individual strengths and circumstances. Yet I still ask: Would I serve Him better as a Jew, or has He placed me here to fulfill a unique role?

Ultimately, I leave this decision in G-d's hands. If He opens the doors and provides the opportunity for me to convert, I will follow that path with devotion. If He keeps me as I am, I will embrace this life with trust in His wisdom. Whatever G-d's plan may be, I accept it wholeheartedly, knowing that His will is perfect and that He has placed me exactly where I am meant to be.

5. How has following this path changed your life?

Following the Noahide path has profoundly transformed my life, shaping how I view relationships, community, and my sense of purpose. On a personal level, it has taught me to prioritize respect, compassion, and recognizing the Divine image in every person. This mindset has deepened my relationships, allowing me to approach disagreements with greater patience and understanding.

In my friendships, the Noahide principles have encouraged me to live with fairness and accountability. These values are not abstract ideals but guide my daily interactions, fostering trust and integrity. Within my broader community, the Noahide mission has inspired me to promote ethical and just environments.

I work to spread awareness of the Seven Noahide Commandments and foster a supportive community. Through writing blog posts, translating Noahide books, and organizing events with guest speakers, I aim to reach and inspire as many people as possible. Sharing this perspective with others has been a meaningful way to connect and create positive change.

This path has also given me a renewed sense of purpose. Translating the Noahide principles into tangible actions, like promoting kindness and fairness, has allowed me to inspire curiosity about this way of life without imposing my beliefs on others.

The Seven Laws have also reshaped how I define success. Instead of measuring achievements solely by worldly standards,

I now focus on how closely my actions align with Divine values. This perspective has brought a deep sense of peace and fulfillment, knowing that my efforts contribute to a greater purpose beyond myself.

6. What are you currently learning?

I'm continuing to deepen my understanding and practice of the Seven Laws of Noah, exploring not only their foundational principles but also their broader implications for daily life and personal growth. These Laws provide a clear, accessible framework for living a moral and righteous life, transcending cultural and religious boundaries. They emphasize core values such as justice, kindness, and accountability, which resonate deeply with the shared human experience.

One of the most profound realizations I've had is that the Seven Laws are not just rules, they are a way to align with G-d's will for all humanity. They have helped me appreciate that G-d cares for all people, providing everyone with the tools to live meaningful and ethical lives. This inclusivity has given me a renewed sense of purpose and connection to humanity as a whole.

Another essential part of my learning has been understanding the distinction between the unique covenant G-d has with the Jewish people and the universal mission of the Noahide Laws. The Seven Laws are not about adopting someone else's identity but about fulfilling the role G-d has set for each individual. This perspective has allowed me to embrace my spiritual identity with authenticity and humility, honoring G-d's design for humanity.

My studies have also reinforced the importance of lifelong learning. The Seven Laws, while seemingly straightforward, carry layers of meaning that deepen with continued study and reflection. Delving into texts such as *The Divine Code* and engaging in discussions with rabbis and fellow Noahides has revealed new insights and applications, making the journey one of constant growth and discovery.

Finally, I've learned that living according to the Seven Laws is not about perfection but about progress. It is a continuous journey of striving to do better, to treat others with dignity, and to make choices that align with G-d's moral blueprint. This ongoing effort has enriched my life with a sense of purpose and fulfillment that grows deeper with time.

7. How do you apply what you learn to your daily life?

Applying the principles of the Seven Laws of Noah has transformed how I live and interact with the world. These laws serve as a moral compass, guiding my decisions and shaping my relationships. They remind me daily of the importance of integrity, compassion, and accountability in every action I take.

Within my family, I strive to foster an environment rooted in kindness and respect. I teach my children the values of fairness, honesty, and empathy, using the Seven Laws as a foundation for their moral education. By modeling these principles in my own behavior, I aim to inspire them to lead lives of integrity and purpose.

In my community, I work to promote ethical living and mutual understanding. I have participated in interfaith dialogues, sharing the Noahide perspective with people from different backgrounds. These interactions have helped bridge gaps and build connections, emphasizing the universal values that unite us all. Additionally, I volunteer my time to support local initiatives that align with the principles of justice and kindness, such as programs for underprivileged families and community-building projects.

On a personal level, I use the Seven Laws to navigate ethical dilemmas in my daily life. Whether it's making decisions in my professional work or resolving conflicts in relationships, I turn to these principles as a guide. They help me stay grounded and ensure that my actions reflect my commitment to living according to G-d's will.

Finally, I embrace the importance of personal accountability. The Noahide path emphasizes that each individual has a role to play in making the world a better place. By taking responsibility for my actions and striving to align them with the Seven Laws, I have found a sense of peace and fulfillment. This daily practice has not only enriched my spiritual life but also strengthened my connection to others and my sense of purpose in the world.

KEY LESSONS

1. **True faith requires questioning and growth.** I had to question everything I was taught, even when it felt like my world was unraveling. Faith isn't about accepting what others say, it's about seeking truth, even when uncomfortable. Every challenge and contradiction pushed me closer to clarity and a real relationship with G-d.

2. **Spiritual transformation comes through life's hardest trials.** My mother's illness and passing were some of the hardest moments of my life, but they forced me to confront deep moral questions. In that struggle, I found strength to seek answers beyond what I had been told. The pain shaped me and led me to the Seven Laws of Noah and a deeper understanding of G-d's will.

3. **G-d's plan is universal yet personal.** Learning about the Seven Laws showed me that G-d has a plan for all humanity, and for me personally. Though Judaism has a unique covenant, I realized my role is just as meaningful. G-d created me for a purpose, fulfilled through the Noahide path.

4. **Spiritual identity is a journey, not a fixed destination.** I struggled for a long time, wondering if I should become Jewish or serve G-d as a Noahide. Over time, I realized I don't need to rush to define my path. What matters is living with sincerity, following G-d's will, and trusting Him to guide me.

5. **Living by G-d's Laws shapes every aspect of life.** The Seven Laws of Noah aren't just abstract; they guide my daily life. From how I treat others to how I carry myself in the world, these laws give me a clear moral foundation. The more I align with them, the more peace and purpose I find.

6. **The search for truth requires persistence and openness.** I didn't discover the Seven Laws overnight, it took years of questioning, studying, and admitting when I was wrong. Letting go of old beliefs was painful, but each step brought me closer to truth. Real growth comes from staying open, even when answers challenge what I once believed.

7. **Our purpose is to reflect Divine values in the world.** Everything I do, how I treat people, study, and share, brings G-d's truth into the world. I no longer feel the need to convince others; I focus on living by example. My purpose is to bring light wherever I can, and that's the most meaningful work I can do.

7.

Daisy Catherina | (Singapore)

EMBRACING FAITH AND RESILIENCE

"Life becomes profoundly meaningful when we see every challenge as a lesson from Hashem and every moment as an opportunity for gratitude."

1. What is your background?

My name is Daisy Catherina, and I was born in Indonesia. I learned English while studying in the U.S., which has greatly helped me in life. After completing my studies in China, I felt that returning to Indonesia would not allow me to use my language skills effectively. So, I moved to Singapore, where I've lived ever since.

In Singapore, I was an active Christian. I joined a church, formed friendships, and participated in a Bible study group led by a Singaporean family. It was during this time that my spiritual journey began to take a different turn.

2. How did you discover the Seven Laws of Noah?

During one of our Bible study sessions, the leader suggested starting with Genesis and exploring the Hebrew roots of the Bible. The deeper we dug, the more we realized how much we didn't know. This curiosity led us to explore Messianic Christianity.

Around this time, I learned that Rabbi Brody from Israel was coming to Singapore. In May 2013, I had the opportunity to meet him during *Shemittah*[21]. Although I couldn't attend his evening talk because I had just had a baby, I met him in the afternoon, and he gave me a blessing. That encounter opened the door to learning about the Seven Noahide Laws and changed my spiritual path forever.

I began learning through online resources like Chabad.org and Rabbi Shalom Arush's teachings. I listened to CDs, read books, and slowly immersed myself in the Noahide journey.

3. What impact did this knowledge have on you?

Before discovering the Noahide Laws, I struggled with many unanswered questions from my Christian upbringing. The concept of the Trinity never made sense to me, and I felt restless and insecure. Learning about the Seven Noahide Laws gave me clarity and a sense of peace.

One of the most significant changes has been my approach to gratitude. Jewish teachings emphasize mindfulness and modesty, which have transformed how I see the world and my interactions with others. I've also gained a deeper sense of purpose, especially through the concept of *tikkun olam*[22]. In my work as a Pilates instructor, I help people heal their bodies, which I now see as a form of gratitude and service to Hashem.

4. What has been your biggest challenge?

One of my biggest challenges has been navigating relationships and identity. As a Noahide, I am part of a very small minority, and explaining this path to others, including my children, can be difficult. They sometimes struggle to identify themselves when asked questions about religion or beliefs.

---

21. A Sabbatical year in the Hebrew calendar.
22. Hebrew for "repairing the world".

Additionally, living in Singapore, where the Jewish community is small and security around synagogues is strict, I don't have frequent opportunities to connect with other Noahides or Jews in person. This can feel isolating at times.

5. How has following this path changed your life?

This journey has completely changed how I view life. As a Christian, I often felt restless and unsure of my purpose. Now, I feel much more secure and grounded in myself. Judaism's emphasis on gratitude and structure has provided me with a sense of peace I never had before.

In the fitness industry, where I work, I've adopted Jewish principles of modesty and mindfulness. These values resonate with my clients and have helped build trust. For example, many women feel comfortable bringing their husbands to my Pilates sessions because of how I carry myself.

The way I interact with challenges has also shifted. Whether it's personal struggles or professional setbacks, I now view them as opportunities to grow and refine myself.

6. What are you currently learning?

Right now, I am focused on learning Hebrew because so much of the Torah's depth is in the original language. I take Hebrew lessons every two weeks and study with Rabbis like Avraham Greenbaum and Pinchas Winston, whose teachings help me connect with the timeless wisdom of Judaism.

I also enjoy studying the lives of the *tzadikim*[23] and exploring their stories. These narratives inspire me to persevere through difficulties and cling to faith in Hashem's plan. Additionally, I reg-

---

23. Renown completely righteous people in Jewish history.

ularly read the *Living Emuna* series, which helps me apply the Torah's teachings to my daily life.

7. How do you apply what you learn to your daily life?

I strive to live a life of gratitude and mindfulness, applying the lessons I learn to my work and interactions. The Jewish teachings about modesty and boundaries guide how I conduct myself as a Pilates instructor, fostering trust and respect with my clients.

I also find meaning in everyday moments by incorporating prayers and blessings into my routine. I recite morning prayers from the Jewish *siddur*[24], which remind me to thank Hashem for the simple miracles of life, like movement and health.

Through this journey, I've learned to see challenges not as obstacles, but as opportunities to grow and refine my character. Whether I'm helping someone heal their body or navigating family life, I try to approach everything with gratitude and faith in Hashem's plan.

---

24. The name in Hebrew for the traditional Jewish prayerbook.

KEY LESSONS

1. **Gratitude transforms everything.** I've learned that every challenge, every blessing, and even every breath is a gift from Hashem. When I began to approach life with gratitude, my perspective changed. No matter the circumstances, I now see the hidden blessings and embrace each moment with appreciation.

2. **Faith brings true security.** Before discovering the Noahide path, I often felt restless and uncertain. Now, my faith in Hashem gives me a strong sense of security. Knowing that everything is part of His Divine plan allows me to face life's ups and downs with trust and inner peace.

3. **Challenges are opportunities for growth.** Life's difficulties are not roadblocks; they are lessons designed to refine me. Whether I struggle with relationships, self-doubt, or unexpected setbacks, I remind myself that Hashem places these challenges before me so I can grow, learn, and become a better version of myself.

4. **Modesty and mindfulness create sacred spaces.** Modesty is not just about clothing; it extends to speech, actions, and even thoughts. By practicing mindfulness and respecting boundaries, I cultivate an atmosphere of dignity and trust, both in my personal life and in my work as a Pilates instructor.

5. ***Tikkun olam* begins with small acts of kindness.** Repairing the world isn't about grand gestures; it's about how I treat others every day. Whether I am helping someone heal their body, speaking words of encouragement, or simply showing kindness, I contribute to making the world a better place.

6. **Jewish wisdom provides timeless guidance.** The wisdom of Torah and the stories of the *tzadikim* offer profound insights for modern life. By studying these teachings, I learn how to navigate challenges, make ethical choices, and stay true to my values amidst a constantly changing world.

7. **The journey of learning never ends.** Every new discovery deepens my faith and strengthens my understanding. Whether I'm studying Hebrew, exploring Torah concepts, or reflecting on the lives of *tzadikim*, I realize that learning is a lifelong journey that continually brings me closer to Hashem.

8.

Stefan ben Noah | (Belgium)

LEAVING ILLUSIONS BEHIND

"This journey has taught me that wisdom isn't about knowing everything; it's about learning how to discern truth from illusion."

1. What is your background?

I have always been a critical thinker, someone who questions things and searches for truth. I enjoy analyzing ideas deeply and looking beyond the surface. I was raised in a secular environment but received both religious education and ethics classes in school. These two perspectives, faith and reason, existed side by side, however I never fully connected to either.

When I entered the workforce, I quickly found my job uninspiring and longed for something with more meaning. That led me to explore spirituality and esoteric teachings. I met people who claimed to have deep wisdom and knowledge of spiritual texts, and at first, their ideas fascinated me. However, over time, I realized that much of what they said was vague and detached from reality. Instead of finding clarity, I felt I was getting lost in abstract concepts that didn't hold up under scrutiny.

Eventually, I decided to turn to the Catholic Church, thinking I might find stability there. I also attended an evangelical church briefly, but I couldn't take it seriously. Even within Catholicism, I felt that the teachings lacked depth. Their messages were often limited to "Do your best, work hard," but rarely went beyond that. I wanted something more concrete, something that could stand up to rational thought while still offering spiritual depth.

2. How did you discover the Seven Laws of Noah?

My journey toward the Noahide path began with a personal turning point. About twenty-three years ago, I was taking medication that made reading and retaining information difficult. Even though I didn't feel deeply connected to it, I kept going to church because I was searching for more meaning. As I gradually reduced the medication, my curiosity came back and so did my ability to read.

I first started reading books by secular Jewish authors such as Thomas Friedman, Naomi Klein and Naomi Wolf. At some point, I realized how little I actually knew about the origins of Christianity and the historical Jesus. That led me to *Zealot* by Reza Aslan, an Iranian religious scholar living in the U.S. The book revealed aspects of Jesus' life I had never learned in the Catholic Church, like the fact that he had siblings. It was a major revelation.

After that, I stopped attending church altogether. My interest shifted toward Judaism, and through Facebook, I came across Dutch-language Jewish television. That's where I first heard about Noahides. A rabbi explained that one doesn't need to convert to Judaism to live a meaningful spiritual life. That idea resonated and stayed with me.

3. What impact did this knowledge have on you?

Discovering the Noahide path gave me the sense of direction I had been missing. I've always been drawn to deeper understanding, but I lacked a solid foundation. Now, I have one. My thoughts are clearer, and I feel a stronger connection to meaningful learning.

It has also reshaped how I view morality and ethics. In the past, I often felt that moral teachings were either too vague or too rigid. The Seven Noahide Laws provide a balanced framework, one that is logical, applicable to real life, and based on universal principles rather than cultural traditions.

n practical terms, this understanding has also changed the way I engage with information. I have become more selective about what I read and whom I listen to. In the past, I would dive into any book that seemed intellectually stimulating, even when it lacked real substance. Now, I look for sources that carry integrity and real wisdom.

I frequently come across books, lectures, or rabbis online that spark further study. This ongoing discovery process has enriched my life. It has given me structure and a way to grow intellectually and spiritually.

4. What has been your biggest challenge?

One of the biggest challenges has been finding like-minded people. Noahides form a small and scattered community, which is very different from Christianity, where churches provide a built-in social structure.

At first, I felt very isolated. I didn't personally know anyone who was following this path, and that made it difficult to grow. Unlike in the church, where you can walk into a service and instantly feel part of a group, Noahides don't have that same communal structure. It took me a long time to connect with others who shared my perspective.

I also had to navigate misinformation. There are many people online who claim to teach about the Noahide Laws, but not all of them are reliable. Some mix in their own interpretations, which can be misleading. I had to learn to be cautious and discerning about whom I listened to. Over time, I found trusted sources and a small but solid group of people I can learn from and with.

Another challenge was reconciling my past with my present. While not raised in it, I did spend many years in the Catholic Church, and I was very familiar with its traditions. I used to attend mass in Antwerp, where a pastor I respected led the services. I now see that the teachings of the church don't align with the truth I have come to understand. Letting go of old beliefs and social connections has been a slow process.

5. How has following this path changed your life?

One of the most profound changes is my heightened awareness of life's signals. I can assess situations more clearly and recognize when to avoid certain paths. I feel like I see things more sharply now. I've also experienced unexpected moments of help and guidance when I've asked for it.

My social anxiety has significantly decreased since becoming a Noahide. I even tried to stop taking antidepressants, but the withdrawal symptoms are too uncomfortable. Still, I no longer believe I truly need the medication.

Overall, I've become more positive. My family often complains about politics and world issues, but I find that these things don't weigh on me as much anymore. I enjoy life more and focus on what I can control.

I've made lifestyle changes too. I quit smoking, cut back on TV, and learned to appreciate quiet moments. On the seventh day, I'll have a glass of wine, but I no longer drink during the week.

6. What are you currently learning?

For the past three to four years, I've been studying with Rabbi Jacob de Leeuwe. I attempted to learn Hebrew and studied it for a year, but mastering the language required more time than I could realistically commit to.

I also take lessons with Chabad Utrecht, where everything is taught in Dutch, which makes learning much easier for me. I frequently consult books like the Torah (Delft translation), learn *Tanya*[25] and I enjoy listening to *Tehillim*[26] sung in both Hebrew and English.

7. How do you apply what you learn to your daily life?

My wife and daughter don't fully understand my path. They don't engage with it, but when I find moments where my insights are relevant, I share what I've learned with them.

For those interested in the Noahide path, I would advise being patient and cautious. It's not always easy to find resources or communities, and not all rabbis are trustworthy. Finding the right teachers is essential.

At first, my phone's algorithm didn't show me much about Noahide teachings, but now, my social media is filled with information on the subject. Connecting with a Jewish and/or Noahide community, even if only about the Jewish holidays, can be very helpful.

This path has made me a calmer, wiser, and happier person. I hope the Jewish community continues to support Noahides, and I strive to be a good example while continuing to learn from them.

---

25. See Additional Information on pg. 199.

26. The name in Hebrew for the *Book of Psalms*.

KEY LESSONS

1. **Seeking truth requires courage.** I had to break away from familiar beliefs, and challenge what I had been taught, in order to find something that truly resonated with me.

2. **Clarity comes from structured wisdom.** The Seven Noahide Laws provided a moral framework that was logical and applicable to everyday life, unlike the vague or rigid teachings I had encountered before.

3. **Not all knowledge is created equal.** I have learned to be more discerning about the sources I trust, prioritizing wisdom that is well-founded and practical rather than abstract or misleading.

4. **The spiritual path can be lonely.** Unlike organized religions with built-in communities, Noahides are scattered and harder to find, making the journey one that requires self-motivation and patience.

5. **Transformation is gradual.** From overcoming social anxiety to changing my habits, the impact of this path has been a slow yet profound shift toward a more peaceful and intentional life.

6. **Small lifestyle changes create big shifts.** Quitting smoking, drinking less, and embracing quiet moments have deepened my spiritual experience and sense of self-control.

7. **Being an example is more powerful than persuasion.** My family doesn't fully understand my path, but rather than pushing my beliefs on them, I focus on embodying the wisdom I've gained.

9.

Samuel Murillo Hernández | (Colombia)

FROM POLITICAL SERVICE TO SPIRITUAL PURPOSE

"I once thought meaning could only be found in tradition, philosophy, or politics, but I discovered that true purpose comes from aligning my actions with Torah wisdom."

1. What is your background?

I was born into a Seventh-Day Adventist family in Colombia. My parents were deeply committed to their religion, and before I was even born they envisioned me becoming a priest or pastor, and my entire education was shaped around this path. I attended Seventh-Day Adventist schools because my parents believed that any education outside of religious institutions was inadequate.

It wasn't until I was about twelve years old that I started questioning these beliefs. I wondered why we worshipped someone from another country instead of exploring the religions of indigenous South Americans or African traditions, considering my Afro-Colombian heritage. These questions only deepened when I wasn't allowed to play with neighborhood kids on Saturdays because I had to go to church. I began questioning the very foundation of our religion.

When my behavior at school was deemed undisciplined, my parents moved me to a Presbyterian school. This change marked the beginning of my exposure to other perspectives. Eventually, I convinced them to let me attend a public school. There, I experienced a sense of freedom and equality I hadn't felt in private religious schools.

During this period, I developed a fascination with philosophy. A friend introduced me to Nietzsche's *The Antichrist*, which challenged Christian morals and led me to explore other philosophical texts. However, by my last year of high school, I realized life was about more than abstract ideas. University further broadened my perspective, teaching me that even those who were focused on material things, like fashion or consumption, had their own wisdom to share.

2. How did you discover the Seven Laws of Noah?

My journey toward the Seven Laws of Noah was anything but straightforward. It began in 2004 when I received a scholarship to study art history at Havana University in Cuba. Leaving home for the first time, I found myself in a politically charged environment, surrounded by students who were the children of politicians from around the world. Politics dominated every conversation, a subject I knew little about at the time.

Adapting to this new world proved difficult. I had been raised in a strict Seventh-Day Adventist home, where alcohol and social excess were foreign to me. But in Havana, I drifted, prioritizing socializing and drinking over my studies. Eventually, my academic neglect caught up with me, and after two years, I was expelled and sent back to Colombia.

Determined to move forward, I enrolled in a Catholic university to study foreign trade. One day, while in the university library, I came across an announcement for a contest hosted by the State of Israel, commemorating the 100th anniversary of Theodor Herzl. The test focused on Herzl and Zionism, with the grand prize being a trip to Israel and a meeting with the Prime Minister. This unexpected opportunity fascinated me, and I eagerly took the test. However, due to technical issues, I was unable to complete it and lost my chance to win.

Although I didn't travel to Israel, the experience sparked a deep curiosity about Judaism. Soon after, I began receiving weekly emails from the Israeli Embassy in Uruguay, likely because of my participation in the contest. Every Friday afternoon, I would receive messages filled with updates and insights that nurtured my interest in Jewish teachings. However, when I searched for more information online, I was met with an overwhelming amount of antisemitic conspiracy theories, which discouraged me from exploring further.

Life moved on. In 2011, I married, but by 2013, I found myself separated and searching for direction. One day, while visiting a cultural center, I noticed a man wearing a *kippah*[27] and *peyot*[28]. Feeling drawn to him, I introduced myself and mentioned that my father was a Seventh-Day Adventist pastor. He took an interest in my curiosity about Judaism and invited me to a Torah study group, instructing me to bring a small donation for charity.

That invitation set me on a new path. Through this connection, I met an Orthodox Jewish rabbi from New York who was also an artist. Since I had more free time after my separation, I became his driver, and we developed a friendship. He introduced me to a group studying Torah and the Seven Noahide Laws.

These early morning study sessions were transformative. I learned that, as a non-Jew, I could live a meaningful, spiritual life by following the Noahide path, a universal ethical system rooted in

---

27. The word in Hebrew for a Jewish-style skullcap (yarmulke).

28. The word in Hebrew for earlocks, which are a custom observed by some observant Jewish men.

the Torah, without the need for formal conversion. This revelation resonated strongly with me.

Looking back, I see how each step, each encounter, and each challenge led me to the Seven Laws of Noah. It was not a journey I had planned, but rather one that unfolded naturally, guiding me toward a path that aligned with my beliefs and my search for truth.

3. What impact did this knowledge have on you?

Discovering the Seven Laws transformed my spiritual and mental well-being. I began practicing personal prayer, which profoundly impacted me. It was empowering to realize that I could connect with the Almighty in a direct way, without needing to convert or adhere to religious practices that felt disconnected from my own path.

When I encountered Rabbi Lazer Brody's teachings, they became a cornerstone of my spiritual growth. His lessons helped me focus on prayer and Torah study. During the Covid-19 pandemic, I simplified my life, avoiding distractions like social media. I downloaded Rabbi Brody's teachings from Internet cafes and immersed myself in them. His advice on relationships, particularly on finding a soulmate with loyalty and good character, helped me make difficult but necessary decisions in my personal life.

At the same time, I started gaining a deeper appreciation for Divine providence. I had spent years searching for something meaningful, moving through different philosophies and religious traditions, but nothing resonated as deeply as the Seven Laws of Noah. Studying Torah as a Noahide gave me a sense of clarity, and purpose.

Additionally, my connection to Jewish teachings helped me strengthen my relationship with my father. I carefully chose to focus our discussions on shared beliefs rather than points of theological disagreement. This allowed us to bond over the Torah's wisdom, bridging the gap between our perspectives.

Learning about the Seven Laws of Noah also gave me a new outlook on relationships and ethical living. I began making more thoughtful choices in my personal and professional life, striving to align my actions with the values I had discovered. I realized that spirituality isn't just about rituals; it's about how we treat others, how we handle challenges, and how we pursue wisdom with sincerity.

Through this journey, I found a sense of belonging and a deeper understanding of my place in the world. What had once been a search for intellectual knowledge became a profound spiritual transformation, shaping not just my beliefs but also my daily life.

4. What has been your biggest challenge?

Being a Noahide in Colombia comes with unique challenges. Societal norms and religious traditions sometimes create misunderstandings, particularly during holidays like Christmas or New Year's. People often feel pity for me or don't understand why I choose not to celebrate these occasions. Declining invitations can be difficult, as it sometimes offends others.

I also face misconceptions and antisemitic sentiments from some individuals, which can be disheartening. In these moments, I've learned to respond with questions rather than arguments, encouraging people to reflect on their own biases. Despite these challenges, I remain committed to my beliefs.

Professionally, balancing my work in customer service for government-regulated licensing with my spiritual passions has been another hurdle. I long to dedicate more time to spiritual projects, like the YouTube channel I started to share Rabbi Brody's teachings. However, raising three children and managing responsibilities has made it challenging to maintain.

5. How has following this path changed your life?

Following the Noahide path has reshaped how I view the world and interact with others. Rabbi Brody once told me that while I could be an ordinary Jew if I converted, I could be a "wonderful Noahide" by staying on this path. That affirmation resonated and reinforced my belief that this is the right spiritual path for me.

I have also learned the importance of balance and patience. While I dream of creating an independent project or business that aligns with my spiritual values, I've come to accept that this requires time, planning, and faith in the Almighty's guidance.

Interestingly, before fully embracing the Noahide path, I had a brief involvement in politics. After returning from Havana University, I was invited to take on a leadership role for young people in my region. I worked alongside local government initiatives that aimed to improve opportunities for the youth, advocating for policies that would provide better education and resources. At the time, I saw this as a way to create positive change in my community.

However, my growing spiritual awareness made me question the nature of political work. I saw how easily people's intentions could become clouded by personal ambition, and I felt a pull toward a different kind of leadership, one grounded in ethical living and personal transformation rather than political influence. Eventually, I stepped away from the political path, realizing that true change starts with the individual.

Looking back, I see how those experiences shaped me. They taught me the value of service and the importance of maintaining integrity in all endeavors. Now, instead of seeking leadership in a political sphere, I focus on becoming a better person through the wisdom of the Seven Laws of Noah. I aim to live by example, knowing that real impact begins in everyday actions, conversations, and relationships.

6. What are you currently learning?

Right now, I am studying teachings on *emuna* (faith) and the *Likutei Moharan* by Rabbi Nachman of Breslov. I also continue to learn from Rabbi Brody's lectures. His teachings inspire me to live a more meaningful life and deepen my connection with the Almighty.

Beyond spiritual study, I am also focusing on personal development. I have been reflecting on how to strengthen my discipline and consistency, particularly in prayer and daily ethical living.

Another area of interest for me is the relationship between faith and mental well-being. I have found that teachings on *emuna* not only bring spiritual clarity but also help me navigate challenges with resilience. I am learning how trust in Divine providence can reduce anxiety and lead to a more balanced, fulfilling life.

At the same time, I am continuing to refine my long-term goals, including building an independent project that aligns with my values. Whether through writing, media, or community outreach, I want to create something meaningful that bridges spirituality and practical life, showing others the depth and relevance of the Noahide path in today's world.

7. How do you apply what you learn to your daily life?

I incorporate my faith into daily life through personal prayer, often during my bicycle commutes. This practice helps me feel at peace and stay close to the Almighty, even amidst the busyness of work and family responsibilities. These moments of reflection allow me to express gratitude, seek guidance, and strengthen my connection with Hashem in a natural, personal way.

I share teachings through my WhatsApp and Telegram statuses, and through my YouTube channel (@MrSamuelSpanish). This allows me to internalize the wisdom I value while subtly sharing it with others. It's a small way to contribute to spreading the knowledge of the Seven Laws of Noah. Even a simple message or quote can spark curiosity and encourage others to seek deeper truths.

My commitment to this path has also influenced how I interact with others. By responding to ignorance with kindness and curiosity, I aim to inspire reflection and understanding. I have learned that many people hold misconceptions about Judaism and the Noahide path, often due to misinformation or lack of exposure. Instead of confronting these misunderstandings with frustration, I try to approach conversations with patience and wisdom, allowing the truth to speak for itself.

Additionally, I strive to integrate ethical principles into my daily interactions. Whether in business, family life, or casual conversations, I focus on honesty, integrity, and compassion. I see these values as fundamental to living a Noahide life, not just in study, but in action.

Over time, I've realized that small, consistent efforts, whether in prayer, sharing knowledge, or leading by example, can have a meaningful impact. I believe that spreading this wisdom can make the world a better and safer place for everyone, one conversation and one good deed at a time.

KEY LESSONS

1. **Seeking truth requires courage.** Questioning the beliefs I was raised with led me to explore philosophy, history, and faith. True growth comes from asking difficult questions and being willing to follow the answers wherever they lead.

2. **Every step has a purpose.** From my religious upbringing to my academic failures, political involvement, and personal struggles, every experience prepared me for the path I ultimately embraced. Nothing is wasted in a sincere search for truth.

3. **Spirituality is a personal journey.** I learned that I didn't need to convert to Judaism to develop a meaningful relationship with the Almighty. The Noahide path showed me that faith is about personal commitment, not labels or formal affiliations.

4. **Guidance can come from unexpected places.** A university contest, a chance encounter with a rabbi, and even emails from an embassy all played a role in shaping my understanding of faith. When seeking truth, opportunities often appear in surprising ways.

5. **Transformation takes time and effort.** Balancing faith, work, and family has not always been easy, but I've learned that spiritual growth is a process. Small consistent actions, prayer, study, and ethical living, create a lasting impact over time.

6. **Faith and technology can work together.** Instead of rejecting modern tools, I've found ways to use digital platforms to share wisdom and inspire others. Social media, AI, and online study have become valuable tools in my spiritual journey.

7. **Leading by example is the strongest influence.** I've learned that inspiring change isn't about preaching but about living with integrity. By embodying the values of the Seven Laws of Noah, I can make a difference in the world, one conversation, one action, and one decision at a time.

10.

Eliana bat Noah | (USA)

LISTENING TO THE VOICE

"Trust isn't the absence of fear; it's taking the next step even when the outcome is invisible, knowing that Hashem will provide."

1. What is your background?

For most of my life, I didn't realize what a spectacular childhood I had. I grew up surrounded by a huge extended family. Summer reunions with aunts, uncles, and cousins were central to my life, shaping my values and character. Our family was deeply Christian, with roots going back to my great-grandfather, a circuit-riding preacher in the early 1900s. He traveled with pack mules, setting up revival tents, and was a masterful storyteller. My maternal and paternal grandfathers were both founding deacons of their churches, even helping build the physical structures. Church was a central part of my upbringing; we attended every service, meeting, and event.

When I was about eight, my dad retired from the Navy and entered Bible College, which led to family discussions about theology. Theological discussions between my father and great-grandfather captivated me, even as a child.

When I was around twelve, my dad became a pastor, and our family's role in the church intensified. I became involved in student leadership through the Christian day-school we attended as well as the church youth group. I loved visitation on Saturdays, where we'd knock on doors and invite strangers to church. While my brother found it terrifying, I felt it gave my life purpose. Around that age, my faith became deeply personal, and I developed a passion for evangelism. I dreamed of being a missionary, although societal expectations limited girls to being missionary wives or nurses.

Reading became another passion, both for competition with my sister and as a way to explore my curiosity. I read through the Bible repeatedly, often with commentaries, and began noticing unanswered questions. For example, *Leviticus* mentions sacrifices performed "as instructed," but the specific instructions weren't in the text. Decades later, I discovered that my early questions had unknowingly aligned with a Torah path.

2. How did you discover the Seven Laws of Noah?

I was in my twenties and going through one of the most difficult and isolating times of my life. I was falsely accused of something that led to the loss of my family, friends, and every support system I had. I found myself completely alone, grappling with feelings of abandonment and betrayal. Isolation tends to push me into deep introspection, and this period was no different. I spent a lot of time in prayer, asking profound questions about life and purpose, like, *Who do I be? How do I be?* I was desperate for answers.

During one of these prayers, something extraordinary happened. A voice in my mind spoke to me, a voice I have heard throughout my life. Growing up Christian, I was taught this voice was G-d or the "Holy Spirit", but I've never fully understood it. Is it the *yetzer tov*[29]? Is it the *yetzer hara*?[30] Is it Hashem communi-

29. The term in Hebrew for a person's "good inclination".

30. The term in Hebrew for a person's "bad inclination".

cating directly? I still don't have a clear answer, but I know this: the voice has always been truthful. When I listen to it, my life aligns, and when I don't, things fall apart.

This time, the voice told me: *Be a moral person, do good, and honor Me; that's all there is.* This was a terrifying moment because it went against what I'd been taught all my life about how to be right with G-d. I didn't fully understand what it meant at the time, but it planted the seeds of something much bigger.

For a long time, I wrestled with the concept of this voice. In Christianity, people often say, *G-d told me this,* or *G-d told me that,* but among Jews, this idea is often dismissed or treated with a lot of skepticism. What I heard wasn't prophecy or revelation, but it was deeply personal guidance that I couldn't deny.

It wasn't until much later that I started searching for answers, not just about what it meant to live morally but also about the nature of G-d and my relationship with Him. It was shortly after my fortieth birthday that I prayed a very specific prayer. I was sitting on the balcony looking up at the night sky and having a little "chat" with Hashem. I expressed my confusion over what I read in the Christian Bible and what I had been taught. Sadly, far too many times, those scriptures had been used to excuse manipulation and abuse or shift blame onto me. I would open my Bible to read, but could only hear the voices of those who had used scriptures to their own advantages. I told Hashem that what I wanted to know when I was reading scripture was, who were You talking to? How did they understand what You were saying? How did they then live that out? Little did I know that the answer to this prayer would change my life and the very core of my belief system.

Shortly afterward a pop-up ad began appearing every time I opened my browser, for Aish.com. What's an Aish I'd wonder as I clicked the ad closed. After a few days that little voice instructed me to click on the ad. I did and was surprised to discover a Jewish website that provided free studies on Bible portions. I began to devour the studies and at first only saw the Jewishness of Jesus. Sometime later I discovered the website Chabad.org. My studies deepened, but now I was having questions about the disparities I was seeing in the Jewish teachings and what I had been taught as a Christian. This continued for a few years then one day I ran across some audio teaching by Rabbi Tovia Singer. He is an American Orthodox rabbi and the founder and director of Outreach Judaism, an international organization that focuses on preventing Jews from converting to other faiths, and reclaiming those who have already converted. I was listening to a series that laid out how Christianity had changed Torah, the very words spoken by Hashem, and why Jesus could not be the Messiah. I remember asking myself, if Jesus is not the Messiah, then what is G-d's salvation plan? I was shocked when I turned on the next audio in the series and Rabbi Singer opened by asking, if Jesus is not the Messiah, then what is G-d's salvation plan? And then he explained about *teshuvah*[31] and our personal responsibility for being moral people and connecting to Hashem through the observance of *mitzvot*[32].

I didn't know about the Seven Noahide Laws at the time, but this experience began to shape how I approached life. I continued exploring Jewish teachings, and eventually, I came across the Noahide Laws. It was like a light-bulb moment. These commandments felt like the framework I had been searching for, a clear, simple, and deeply meaningful guide for living a moral life in alignment with Hashem.

---

31. The word in Hebrew for the process of sincere repentance.
32. The word in Hebrew for commandments (sing. *mitzvah*).

Looking back, I can see how Hashem had been preparing me for this path all along. It was as if all my unanswered questions were paving the way for me to discover a Torah path.

3. What impact did this knowledge have on you?

Learning about the Seven Noahide Laws completely upended my worldview while also setting me free. It felt like my entire belief system, my core foundation was dismantled, and everything I thought I knew unraveled. At the same time, my life circumstances were incredibly difficult. I was facing grief, loss, and isolation, and on top of that, Christian friends accused me of "denying Jesus," that I was an apostate, and my struggles were a punishment for turning away from him. Those accusations hurt deeply and added to the challenges I was already facing.

One of the hardest parts of this journey was listening to Rabbi Tovia Singer's teachings. He exposed theological inconsistencies in Christianity that I hadn't noticed before. I now embraced the newfound truths with joy as I realized I had been carrying a lot of shame and guilt from the Christian teachings I grew up with. Christianity often framed suffering as a direct result of sin, which created a harmful cycle of shame and blame. Letting go of that mindset was difficult but ultimately freeing.

For example, I approach my children's struggles very differently now. Instead of saying, "*This is happening because you're not going to church,*" I help them reflect on their choices and explore what they were trying to achieve. I often incorporate tools like cognitive behavioral therapy, which focuses on changing thought patterns, to help them process their experiences without falling into guilt or self-punishment.

The church wasn't equipped to support me during my struggles, especially back then. Mental health issues were stigmatized, and therapy was seen as "satanic." Psychiatric medications were considered demonic. I trained as a lay counselor during that time and was shocked by how much harmful doctrine was woven into the teachings. Even today, I see Christian counselors perpetuating the idea that suffering indicates unrepentant sin, which can be incredibly damaging.

Despite all these challenges, following the Noahide Laws has brought me a sense of purpose and alignment with Hashem.

4. What has been your biggest challenge?

Leaving Christianity meant leaving everything I'd ever known. Church wasn't just a place of worship, it was my entire life. It was my family, my friends, my school, and my social world. When I left, I lost all of that. It felt like I had stepped into a vast void with no structure or community to fall back on.

This sense of isolation wasn't just physical, it was spiritual as well. Most Noahides don't have the equivalent of a church where you can go every week to worship, sing, and connect with others. I deeply missed the music and the immersive worship experiences. There's something so powerful about singing and being surrounded by people who share your faith. Losing that was painful.

Another challenge was finding guidance. When I first started this journey, resources for Noahides were scarce. The fear of creating a "new religion" meant there wasn't much structure for people like me. It took years to find rabbis and communities that could help me navigate this path. Today, I'm grateful for resources like Asknoah.org and the support Chabad provides to Noahides, but those didn't exist when I began.

For many Noahides, leaving Christianity also means losing their families. While I was already somewhat estranged from mine, I've seen others experience the heartbreak of being disowned or ostracized. Even now, there's still a sense of loneliness that comes with this path, especially when it comes to discussing spiritual principles. You can't just go to a local Noahide congregation and engage in those kinds of conversations.

5. How has following this path changed your life?

Following the Seven Noahide Laws has transformed every aspect of how I live and see the world. It's given me a new perspective on morality, personal and social responsibility, and the significance of my actions.

One of the most impactful lessons came from studying the commandment *not to steal.* A rabbi once explained that answering a personal phone call at work, when you're on the clock, is essentially stealing time from your employer. That insight made me reevaluate my behavior in ways I had never considered. I began to see how even small, seemingly insignificant actions could have moral implications.

This journey has also deepened my sense of accountability. My relationship with Hashem is now entirely my responsibility, there's no intermediary to rely on. That clarity has been both empowering and humbling. It's helped me approach life with greater intention and purpose, whether it's through blessing food, helping others, or simply being mindful of how I show up in the world.

At the same time, I've grown more patient and empathetic. I no longer judge others harshly. Instead, I recognize that everyone is on their own journey. This perspective has allowed me to approach challenges with kindness and understanding, both toward others and myself.

6. What are you currently learning?

I'm currently focused on two areas: lessons on the book, *The Gate of Trust,* and learning Hebrew. *The Gate of Trust* has been incredibly transformative. It's teaching me how to move from intellectual belief *(emuna)* to active trust *(bitachon)*. Stories like the parting of the Red Sea and Abraham's journey with Isaac have shown me that trust isn't about the absence of fear; it's about taking the next step, even when the outcome is uncertain.

For example, Israelites had to step into the Red Sea before it parted, demonstrating their trust in Hashem. Similarly, Abraham and Isaac continued forward up that mountain, even through tears, trusting Hashem's plan. These lessons have helped me embrace uncertainty and lean into trust, which has been a challenge for me since safety hasn't always been a constant in my life.

Learning Hebrew has been another long-time goal. Diving into the language has deepened my connection to Jewish teachings and allowed me to engage with sacred texts in a more meaningful way. It's been a powerful way to ground myself on this path.

7. How do you apply what you learn to your daily life?

My recent move to Bend, Oregon, though temporary, has been one of the biggest applications of trust in my life. I didn't have anything concrete, no written guarantees that everything would work out, but I took the step anyway. I trusted Hashem to provide, and He has. While my living situation is modest and inconvenient, I have everything I need: a safe place to sleep, food, clothing, and transportation. Each day, I focus on that next small step in front of me, and what I need for that day manifests. It feels like manna from Heaven.

This experience has completely reshaped my perspective. I've learned to focus on the Creator of the waves, not the waves themselves. When I do that, I find peace and joy, regardless of my circumstances. Even when I face uncertainty, I trust that Hashem will provide what I need.

This trust influences everything, from how I approach work to how I engage with others and advocate for justice in my community. For example, as part of the seventh Noahide commandment[33], I feel a responsibility to speak out against unjust laws and systems. Following this path has given me clarity, purpose, and a sense of why I am here at this specific time and place.

33. The commandment for a society to establish just laws and courts.

KEY LESSONS

1. **The power of trust.** I've learned that true trust in Hashem isn't about being fearless, it's about taking the next step despite my fears, knowing that the Creator has a plan. Trust is an active process, requiring me to lean into faith and take action even when the outcome is uncertain.

2. **Embracing uncertainty.** Some of the most transformative growth I've experienced has come from stepping into the unknown and trusting Hashem to provide. Like Nachshon stepping into the Red Sea before it parted, I've learned that faith requires action, even when I can't see the path ahead.

3. **Moral accountability.** I now see that every action, no matter how small, carries weight. Living a life of integrity means aligning even my smallest choices with moral principles. I recognize that ethical decisions extend beyond major life choices and into my daily interactions. This awareness has heightened my sense of responsibility in everything I do.

4. **Personal responsibility.** I've realized that my spiritual growth begins when I take full ownership of my relationship with Hashem, without relying on intermediaries. This understanding has empowered me to forge a direct and meaningful connection with my faith, rather than waiting for others to define it for me.

5. **Finding freedom in Laws.** I once saw commandments as restrictions, but now I see the Seven Noahide Laws as a framework that elevates my daily life. Instead of limiting me, they give me a structure for ethical and spiritual growth, helping me find deeper meaning in every moment.

6. **Patience and empathy.** I've come to understand that everyone is on their own journey. This has helped me let go of judgment and approach life's challenges, both my own and others', with greater compassion. Practicing kindness and patience has allowed me to create space for personal and communal growth.

7. **Listening to the voice.** The inner voice that aligns with truth and righteousness has always been a guiding force in my life. I've learned to discern and follow it, knowing that when I do, my life moves in alignment with Hashem's will. Trusting this voice has given me clarity, purpose, and a deeper sense of connection to the path I am meant to walk.

11.

Justin Sprueill | (USA)

SEEKING ANSWERS, FINDING G-D

"I no longer feel obligated to persuade people. Instead, I let my actions reflect my beliefs and let others come to their own conclusions."

1. What is your background?

I was raised in a suburban, predominantly white, pseudo-Christian environment. My father came from a deeply religious background but didn't take it seriously until later in life. My mother was involved with a Seventh-day Adventist-like group, almost cult-like. This created conflicts in their approach to raising me in religious matters, which they only truly pursued when I was nearly a teenager.

At that time, they doubled down on religious education, enrolling me in a Christian discipleship high school. Later, I pursued college and ended up earning four associate degrees just trying to qualify for a nursing program. Eventually, I attended a Christian college where I minored in Bible studies. However, my faith was never firm, I believed in G-d, but the tenets of Christianity never fully resonated with me. My doubts only deepened with formalized education because I had questions that never received satisfactory answers.

One of the biggest issues for me was the Nicene Creed, I found it abhorrent that fundamental theological disputes were settled by vote. I also struggled with the contradictions between Paul and Jesus, as well as the concept of the Holy Spirit as a distinct entity. Many of the answers I received felt circular or dismissive.

Despite going through Christian education, I continued to study spirituality on my own, listening to apologetics podcasts and engaging in discussions. One of these podcasts suggested choosing a single book of the Bible to study deeply rather than trying to read the entire text in a year. I chose *Isaiah,* as it was a book I had spent the least time with. I read it through multiple times, incorporating commentary. For the first time, I decided to seek a Jewish perspective, reasoning that Jews had been studying these texts for millennia and likely had deeper insights. That's when I came across Rabbi Tovia Singer's teachings.

2. How did you discover the Seven Laws of Noah?

About six hours into Rabbi Singer's commentary on Isaiah, everything clicked for me. It resolved all of my theological struggles, the conflict between Paul and Jesus, the nature of the Holy Spirit, and more. The realization was overwhelming: by removing Jesus from the equation and looking at the *Tanach*[34] in its original context, everything made sense.

From there, I started learning as much as I could about Judaism, listening to podcasts and lectures. This shift happened around late 2019 or early 2020. At first, I was hesitant to talk to my wife, Melissa, about it because I wasn't sure how she would react. But to my surprise, she was very open and supportive, and I'm really grateful for that.

Initially, I was focused more on disproving Christianity than embracing a new belief system. The concept of Noahides came

34. The name in Hebrew for the 24 Books of the Hebrew Bible. See fn. 3.

later, either through Rabbi Singer's teachings or other related sources. My initial goal was simply to leave Christianity, not necessarily to take on a new identity. Over time, I discovered organizations like Brit Olam and other Noahide communities.

Melissa went through a Messianic phase while she was still Christian, which made me wary because I already understood that we shouldn't be forming our own hybrid religion. It took time for both of us to fully grasp the structure and limitations of the Noahide path.

3. What impact did this knowledge have on you?

Initially, my journey out of Christianity was more academic than spiritual. I was always interested in philosophy and anarchism, so I treated religion as another subject of study. My parents' late entry into serious religious practice didn't make it foundational for me growing up. However, once I started questioning things deeply, I became more engaged.

The biggest change has been how I study scripture. In my Christian education, I had a bad habit of reading my own feelings and ideas into everything. Now, I approach it with more humility, seeing the text as something to learn from rather than something to shape to fit my own perspective.

Another major change is my awareness of modesty, both in behavior and interactions with others. Christianity often promotes a carefree approach; Luther even said, "Sin boldly because you are forgiven." Judaism, and by extension the Noahide path, does not operate that way. I've become much more conscientious in my daily interactions.

Additionally, my relationship with Hashem has become more structured and intentional. Instead of relying on faith alone, I now have a clear moral and intellectual framework to guide my decisions.

4. What has been your biggest challenge?

A significant challenge has been the sense of loneliness. While there are Noahide communities, we are discouraged from forming our own distinct religious movement. This often leaves us in a spectator role rather than being fully integrated into Jewish communities. Additionally, I struggle with knowing what I am permitted to study. Talmudic teachings and Midrashic interpretations are largely restricted for non-Jews,[35] so I have to be careful not to overstep.

We incorporate Torah into daily life as much as possible. The kids see my wife, Melissa, practicing modesty, and they experience Jewish values in our home. However, holidays are tricky because there's a fine line between respectful participation and overstepping. Community is essential to Judaism, and being outside of it makes practicing much harder.

Identity is another challenge. We haven't explicitly told our children that we are distinct from Jews, but as they grow, that conversation will need to happen.

Friends know to varying degrees, but I generally say, "I practice Judaism," as a shorthand. Most people don't ask further. My family, however, does not know explicitly. They see that we choose not to eat pork nor celebrate Christmas, but I haven't had a direct conversation with them. Given their heavy investment in Christian education for me, it would likely cause major conflict.

5. How has following this path changed your life?

It hasn't been difficult for me personally, as I was skeptical of Christian holidays even when I was still in the faith. However, navigating it with children is much harder since schools and media

---

35. See Additional Information, pg. 199.

push these celebrations. Explaining why we don't participate without isolating them is a delicate balance.

I also now have a different perspective on relationships. In Christianity, there was always a focus on converting others. Now, I no longer feel obligated to persuade people. Instead, I let my actions reflect my beliefs and let others come to their own conclusions.

I feel more grounded in my faith than ever before. I no longer have to make excuses for theological inconsistencies, and I have a clear understanding of what is expected of me.

6. What are you currently learning?

I am constantly studying Torah and Jewish teachings to better understand my role as a Noahide. One of my biggest focuses is refining my study habits, learning to engage with Jewish texts without overstepping boundaries.

I also spend a lot of time listening to rabbis and educators to gain insight into ethical living and morality from a Jewish perspective. There's a constant process of growth, and I am always seeking to expand my knowledge.

Beyond that, I am working on balancing my natural skepticism with faith. Some Midrashic stories sound fantastical to me,[36] and I am learning to appreciate them without dismissing them outright.

7. How do you apply what you learn to your daily life?

I try to apply my learning by being intentional in how I interact with the world. I am more mindful of how I treat people, ensuring that my words and actions reflect a higher moral standard.

---

36. In the books of Midrash, the Talmudic sages sometimes concealed deep spiritual teachings by weaving them into allegorical, non-literal stories.

In practical terms, we have incorporated elements of Jewish practice into our daily lives while staying within Noahide guidelines. This includes avoiding *lashon hara*,[37] being more conscious about ethical decision-making, and teaching our children values rooted in Torah.

I also make sure that I continue my studies regularly. Whether through online lectures, discussions with other Noahides, or personal reading, I make a point to keep learning and refining my understanding of the Torah and Hashem's expectations for us.

Ultimately, my goal is to live a life of integrity, humility, and righteousness. This path is not just about following rules; it is about becoming a better person every single day.

37. The term in Hebrew for "sinful speech" which one says about another person (for example, gossip).

KEY LESSONS

1. **I learned that truth requires deep study.** I used to accept religious teachings at face value, assuming they were true because they had been passed down for generations. But when I finally took the time to study, question, and seek original sources, I realized how much I had overlooked. Truth is something I have to actively pursue, it's not just handed to me.

2. **Faith shouldn't be about blind acceptance.** I was always told to "just have faith" whenever I had doubts, but that approach never sat right with me. Now, I understand that real faith is built on knowledge, reasoning, and genuine understanding. I no longer feel pressured to believe in contradictions; I have clarity and confidence in my relationship with Hashem.

3. **Spiritual growth is a process, not an instant transformation.** It took years for me to fully transition from Christianity to where I am now. At first, I was just focused on disproving what I had been taught. It wasn't until later that I truly embraced a new way of living. I've learned that growth happens gradually, and that's alright; every step forward is meaningful.

4. **Integrity matters more than religious labels.** I no longer feel the need to define myself by a specific religious group or prove my faith to others. What matters most is how I live, how I treat people, how I speak, how I handle ethical dilemmas. Following the Noahide path has shown me that righteousness isn't about fitting into a category but about living with integrity every day.

5. **Finding community is crucial to staying strong in this path.** One of the hardest parts of this journey has been feeling isolated. Without a local Jewish or Noahide community, I sometimes feel like I'm on my own. But through online study groups, rabbis, and friends who share my values, I've realized that I'm not alone. Seeking out like-minded people has been a lifesaver.

6. **Living righteously is a daily commitment.** Being a Noahide isn't just about what I believe, it's about what I do. I try to be mindful of my words, avoid gossip, act with kindness, and make ethical choices. Every decision I make is an opportunity to align myself more with Hashem's expectations, and that awareness has changed how I live my life.

7. **I no longer feel the need to convince others; my actions speak for themselves.** In Christianity, I was always taught that spreading the faith was a duty. Now, I understand that I don't need to persuade anyone. Instead, I focus on living in a way that reflects truth and righteousness. If others are curious, they will ask. My goal isn't to convert anyone, it's to live with honesty, humility, and purpose.

12.

Melissa Sprueill | (USA)

A SEARCH FOR TRUTH

"Faith isn't about blind acceptance;
it's about asking questions, seeking answers,
and aligning with truth."

1. What is your background?

I grew up in a deeply Christian home. My dad was Catholic, and my mom was Baptist. For the first ten years of my life, we alternated between a Baptist church and Catholic mass. My dad wanted us to understand his upbringing, so he took us to mass occasionally. But as I grew older, I noticed we were going less frequently, and by the time I was ten, my dad had fully converted to Baptist Christianity. He and my brother were baptized together, solidifying our family's shift in faith.

Church was central to our lives. My parents became very involved, and my dad took on leadership roles, eventually becoming a deacon and leading various committees. We were at church almost every day, attending services, prayer meetings, choir rehearsals, and youth leadership gatherings. I taught Sunday school, sang in the choir, and even worked at the church's school and their Vacation Bible School during the summer. My entire world revolved around our faith community.

I attended Christian schools from kindergarten through high school, except for two years in public school. I returned to

Christian school for my junior and senior years, which is where I met Justin.

2. How did you discover the Seven Laws of Noah?

From a young age, I had a lot of questions, about Jesus, about G-d, about the inconsistencies I noticed in scripture. But whenever I asked, I was met with vague responses. My parents would direct me to the pastor, whose answer was usually, "You just have to have faith." The more I probed, the more I realized that many of the beliefs I had been taught weren't actually in the Bible. For instance, I was told that drinking alcohol was sinful, even though Jesus supposedly turned water into wine. Over time, I learned to suppress my doubts and simply accept things as they were.

Then, Covid changed everything. Without church, I felt disconnected. I started listening to different pastors online, searching for guidance, but something always felt off. In 2022, I told Justin we needed to find a church for our kids. That's when he admitted that he had been struggling with his faith for years. He had long harbored doubts about Paul but had never voiced them.

That moment was pivotal. Justin suggested we each read the Bible independently and search for the truth. I started in the New Testament, as I had been taught, but quickly saw contradictions. Paul's teachings often conflicted with Jesus' words, and even the Gospel accounts didn't align with each other. The deeper I looked, the more I felt my foundation crumbling.

I was terrified. If everything I had believed was wrong, what did that mean for me? What did it mean for my salvation? The fear of hell loomed over me. Then, Justin suggested I listen to Rabbi Tovia Singer. At first, I resisted, I had always been told never to listen to rabbis. But my desire for truth outweighed my fear. I gave it a chance, and suddenly, everything made sense. I fact-checked everything he said against my own Bible, and it was all there. The truth had been in front of me all along, I just hadn't been allowed to see it.

3. What impact did this knowledge have on you?

On November 12, 2022, I repented to Hashem. I felt immense guilt for having spent so many years believing and teaching falsehoods, but at the same time, I was overwhelmed with gratitude for finally knowing the truth. It was as if my entire worldview had shifted overnight.

My relationship with Hashem has deepened in ways I never expected. I no longer feel like I am blindly following rules without understanding. Now, every action I take is deliberate and meaningful. I approach prayer differently, not as a chore or an obligation, but as an intimate conversation with the Creator. I also began to recognize the importance of ethical behavior beyond religious rituals. Being a Noahide is not just a belief. It's about how I live my life, how I treat others, and how I uphold truth and integrity.

4. What has been your biggest challenge?

This journey has not been without challenges. Family resistance has been the hardest. Some relatives assume Justin pressured me into this decision, but in reality, this was my choice. Many people in my life do not understand why I left Christianity, and some have reacted with hostility. There is a big emotional toll in feeling isolated from people I once shared faith with.

I also struggle with isolation, as there is no local Noahide or Jewish community near us. I would love to attend a synagogue, but there simply isn't one close enough. There are also practical challenges; figuring out how to celebrate holidays as a Noahide, navigating kosher food when we aren't required to keep it but want to make conscious dietary choices, and raising our children with a strong sense of faith without a physical community around them.

5. How has following this path changed your life?

Since embracing the Noahide Laws, I have found a deep inner peace. I no longer feel the pressure of trying to force belief in things that never made sense. Instead, I feel aligned with truth and purpose. My family life has also changed, we focus more on kindness, gratitude, and ethical living. We strive to create a home environment that reflects our values and devotion to Hashem.

Another major shift is how I view relationships. Before, I felt a strong obligation to convert others or convince them of what I believed. Now, I recognize that my role is to live by example, not to push beliefs on anyone. I am learning to cultivate relationships based on mutual respect rather than religious agreement.

6. What are you currently learning?

I am constantly expanding my knowledge of Torah and Jewish teachings. I study with Noahide groups and follow various rabbis who provide guidance on living a righteous life. One of my main areas of focus right now is understanding how to bring more spirituality into my daily life, through prayer, study, and ethical behavior.

I am also learning more Hebrew to better understand prayers and Jewish texts. Language is such an important part of faith, and being able to connect with the words of Torah in their original form adds another layer of depth to my studies.

7. How do you apply what you learn to your daily life?

I apply what I learn by being intentional in everything I do. I watch my words more carefully, making sure not to engage in gossip or negativity. I dress modestly as a reflection of my values. I guide my children in learning about Hashem and living with integrity. Even the way I interact with others, family, friends, and strangers, is influenced by my awareness of Hashem's presence in the world.

I also make time for structured study, I am constantly growing and learning. I seek out online classes, listen to lectures, and engage with other Noahides who are on a similar path. I also incorporate small but meaningful practices into my daily routine, such as saying blessings[38], setting aside time for quiet reflection, and practicing gratitude in every aspect of life.

Through this journey, I have come to understand that living as a Noahide is about striving to be a better person each day. This path has given me clarity, and a deep sense of gratitude.

I am so grateful for this path.

---

38. Noahides are encouraged to say blessings to G-d for His creation of the various foods before they eat or drink, and a blessing of thanks to G-d after finishing a meal.

KEY LESSONS

1. **Courage to question leads to growth.** Letting go of everything I was raised to believe was one of the hardest things I've ever done. Questioning meant risking relationships and my sense of identity, but I couldn't ignore the contradictions. True faith isn't about blind acceptance; it's about seeking answers, even when it's uncomfortable.

2. **Faith should be rooted in understanding, not just emotion.** I was always told to "just have faith," but that left me feeling lost. Studying the *Tanach* with an open mind changed my life. Now, my faith is grounded in knowledge, not just emotion, and my relationship with Hashem feels real, not forced.

3. **Challenges are part of growth.** Walking away from Christianity wasn't easy. Some family members blamed my husband, Justin; others reacted with anger. But growth often comes through struggle. Letting go of old beliefs and adjusting to a new way of life is hard, but every challenge has strengthened my convictions.

4. **Community matters, even if it's virtual.** Not having a local Noahide or Jewish community has been difficult, but I've learned that I'm not alone. Online study groups, teachers and friendships with other Noahides have given me the support and guidance I need.

5. **Living by example is more powerful than words.** When I was a Christian, I felt pressured to convert others. Now, I don't need to convince anyone. My responsibility is to live with integrity. If people are curious, they'll ask. True faith isn't about proving anything; it's about embodying what you believe.

6. **Spirituality is a journey, not a destination.** There's no final moment where I've "arrived." I'm always learning, studying, and refining my understanding. This path is about striving each day to be a better person and serve Hashem with sincerity.

7. **Living with intention brings lasting peace.** Since embracing the Noahide path, my life has become more purposeful. I think more about my words, dress modestly, and create a home filled with a feeling of holiness. These choices aren't restrictions; they bring clarity, peace, and a deep sense of fulfillment.

13.

Jecinta Njambi | (Kenya)

TORAH IN KENYA: ONE WOMAN'S SEARCH

My soul didn't feel at home in church or Messianic teachings, but when I found the Seven Laws, it was like something ancient in me finally stood still.

1. What is your background?

I was born in 1976 into a Christian family in Kenya. My grandparents, parents, everyone around me, was Christian. But even as a little girl in Sunday school, I felt something was missing. I went from church to church, always searching. Nothing ever felt right.

At age fifteen, I joined a Messianic group. I thought I had found the truth. I stayed in that movement for many years. But in 2002, something changed when an elder in our church named Humphrey began asking hard questions about doctrine. The leaders accused him of bringing in strange teachings and expelled him. I felt they had treated him unfairly, so I left with him.

Humphrey traveled to Israel to search for the truth. When he returned, he said, "I found nothing solid in that place. But I believe there is something true, only it's far, and we have to work hard to reach it."

2. How did you discover the Seven Laws of Noah?

Humphrey tried to convert to Judaism but was told, "You don't need to become Jewish. As a Gentile, you can serve G-d through the Seven Noahide Laws." This was a shock to all of us. We had never heard of these laws.

He began studying with Dr. Michael Schulman from Ask Noah. After completing the first few classes, he invited us to learn too. At that time, my English was very poor, and I asked, "How can I understand?" He answered, "If you truly wish to follow Hashem, He will open the gates." That answer stayed with me.

We began Course One using *The Path of the Righteous Gentile*[39]. Later, when WhatsApp became available, I was able to communicate directly with Dr. Schulman. He became not just my teacher, but my advisor. I prayed to Hashem that I could stay on this path, and He made a way.

3. What impact did this knowledge have on you?

One of the things that happened was that I began collecting books: *The Divine Code*, *To Perfect the World*[40], *The Five Books of Moses*. If it could bring me closer to Hashem, I wanted it.

My family didn't understand. They thought I had lost my mind for turning away from JC. But I had finally found clarity. I learned that G-d has no body, never dies, and no one is punished for the sins of another. Each of us is responsible for our own actions.

Even when I was the only Noahide in my surroundings, I knew I was finally in the right place. I was no longer wandering.

---

39. The authorized 1987 edition, titled *The Path of the Righteous Gentile: An Introduction to the Seven Laws of the Children of Noah.*

40. *To Perfect the World: The Lubavitcher Rebbe's Call to Teach the Noahide Code to All Mankind*, 2nd Edition, pub. Sichos In English.

4. What has been your biggest challenge?

Marriage. I remained unmarried for many years because I feared being pulled back into Christianity. In 2023, I did marry; my husband is not a Noahide and follows no religion, but he respects my path and supports me.

Another challenge was loneliness. When you leave church, you lose a social world. But Judaism encourages us Noahides not to isolate from family or community. Unlike Christianity and Messianic groups, where we separated ourselves and felt superior, Judaism encourages connection, unity, and peace.

5. How has following this path changed your life?

The teachings of Christianity had made me believe I was better than others. But learning Torah and the Seven Laws taught me otherwise. Even Noah tried to uplift his generation, not separate from them.

I started reconnecting with my family. When my sister passed away, I formed new bonds with her children and husband. That grief taught me the importance of love, unity, and compassion.

People around me noticed. They said, "You're not the same. You come to family events again. You act differently." And it's true. Unless something clearly violates the Seven Laws, I now show up, with peace and warmth.

6. What are you currently learning?

Right now, I'm studying the section on courts and justice in *The Divine Code.* I also read *Psalms* every day, praying for the peace of Jerusalem and the safety of Israel. I learned from *Jerusalem, The Eye of the Universe*[41] that if there's no peace in Jerusalem, there won't be lasting peace anywhere in the world.

---

41. A book by Rabbi Aryeh Kaplan.

Another favorite book is *Perek Shirah*[42]. It teaches how every element of creation, trees, rivers, animals, sings praise to Hashem. That idea fills me with awe.

7. How do you apply what you learn to your daily life?

I wake up early, wash, give charity, and then pray. I thank Hashem for the workings of my body and for giving me life. Throughout the day, I say blessings over food, drink, and beautiful creations, even when I'm farming. Every moment is an opportunity to thank Him.

I try not to speak *lashon hara*, bad speech. A young woman once told me that the moment she stopped gossiping, she found peace. I took that advice to heart. It changed my life.

Even farming has become spiritual. I noticed that weeds grow faster than crops. The *yetzer hara*[43] is like that. It takes constant effort to uproot negativity and cultivate good. But the harvest is worth it.

42.. *Perek Shirah (Chapter of Song)*, is an anonymous ancient Hebrew text in which different elements of creation are each described as "singing" a different verse from the Hebrew Bible. While some traditions ascribe it to King David or King Solomon, scholars place its compilation in the Geonic period (589–1030 in the Common Era) from earlier Midrashic and Talmudic sources.

43. The term in Hebrew for a person's "bad inclination".

KEY LESSONS

1. **Hashem opens the gates when your soul is sincere.** Even when I didn't speak English and had no way to learn, Hashem helped me. I asked, I searched, and He answered.

2. **You don't have to convert to serve G-d.** There is a righteous path for Gentiles. I learned that the Seven Laws are not a lesser path, they are a holy one.

3. **Books are teachers.** Every Torah-based book I found had something to show me. Sometimes, I'd open a book and find exactly the answer I had been searching for.

4. **Family matters.** I once separated myself from others, thinking "holiness" meant isolation. Now I know it means treating others with respect and kindness. I reconnected with my family through this path.

5. **Pain can bring transformation.** Losing my sister hurt deeply. But it opened my heart to love in a way I hadn't before. Suffering can be the start of healing.

6. **Stick to one voice.** In a world of endless opinions, it's easy to get lost. I found stability through one teacher, one guide, and one consistent path.

7. **Every act counts.** From saying a blessing to giving charity or holding back gossip, small acts, repeated daily, create a life in which every moment is an opportunity to serve Hashem.

14.

Fred Flanigan | (USA)

FROM FIRE AND BRIMSTONE TO TIMELESS TRUTH

"Living by the Seven Laws is about trying to do the right thing every day. It's in the small stuff, being honest, showing kindness, treating people with respect."

1. What is your background?

I grew up in the Salvation Army, where fire-and-brimstone preaching was the norm. My grandparents would say things like, "If you do bad, G-d's gonna smite you down." But even as a kid, I noticed that wasn't happening. I could mess up, and G-d didn't strike me down. That was the beginning of my questioning.

Later, I went through the Corps Cadets program, an intensive Bible study focused entirely on the Christian perspective. I had questions even then, ones that didn't have answers. After I married my wife, my partner for forty-five years, I joined her church, the Disciples of Christ. I became a deacon right away, worked up to being an elder, and taught Sunday school for over thirty years.

But no matter how involved I was, one thing never sat right with me: the idea that G-d's eternal Word could change. How could the Old Testament and the New Testament fit together when they seemed to contradict each other? I believe that if G-d's Word isn't eternal, I don't know if I want to serve Him. That struggle is what kept me searching.

2. How did you discover the Seven Laws of Noah?

It all started with a prayer: "G-d, guide me to the truth. Lead me to where I need to be to hear Your voice." I had questions, big ones, and nobody seemed to have the answers.

The first time I heard about the Noahide path was from a surprising place, the guy who cuts my hair. One day, he started talking about it, and something about what he said stuck with me. I couldn't get it out of my mind.

At church, people started calling me the "Old Testament guy" because I was always focused on those books. During one Vacation Bible School, they even had me play a rabbi in a skit. I took it seriously, probably too seriously, but deep down, I felt like I had no business playing that role.

The real turning point came at a Shabbat dinner hosted by Rabbi Tovia Singer in Dallas. I asked a question that had bothered me for years: "If G-d's Word is eternal, why did He tell Noah he could eat any animal, but later tell Moses that only certain animals were permissible?"

Rabbi Singer asked me, "Who was G-d talking to when He spoke to Noah?" "Noah," I answered. "And what religion was Noah?" I hesitated, then said, "A Gentile, there were no Jews yet." Rabbi Singer nodded and explained, "Exactly. The Laws given to Noah were for all humanity. The Laws given to Moses were specifically for the Israelite nation, setting them apart."

That answer was like a lightning bolt. It reframed everything I thought I knew and gave me a clear sense of where I belonged.

3. What impact did this knowledge have on you?

It was a transformative experience, though not without its challenges. I was deeply rooted in Christian traditions growing up, and each of my brothers took their own path when it came to faith, except for Ike, of blessed memory, who became a truck driver. Pat, now Akiva, converted to Orthodox Judaism, even divorcing his wife when she couldn't accept his new beliefs. My brother Mike, of blessed memory, became Yitzchok, and moved his entire family to Israel, where they all converted to Judaism. Meanwhile, Lewis became a Methodist minister.

I didn't convert to Judaism, but I embraced the Noahide Laws. They gave me clarity I'd never experienced before, resolving the contradictions that had troubled me for years. I no longer felt compelled to force the Old and New Testaments to fit together. Instead, I saw that G-d's Word was consistent, with its application varying based on the audience and their covenant with Him. This realization lifted a tremendous weight off my shoulders. I didn't have to adopt beliefs that didn't make sense to me; instead, I could embrace the timeless truths meant for all humanity, as revealed through Noah.

One moment, in particular, solidified my path. While visiting Israel, I stopped by a shop. The shopkeeper asked me questions, and I explained that I was "just a Noahide." He immediately laid into me, saying, "Don't ever say you're 'just' a Noahide! The Noahide Laws are foundational to the world. They're for all humanity. You should be proud of it!" That moment shifted my perspective entirely. I began to see the immense value and purpose in my path, realizing that the Noahide Laws weren't merely a fallback, they were a profound connection to G-d and a meaningful way to live as part of His creation.

4. What has been your biggest challenge?

The greatest challenge has been unlearning decades of ingrained beliefs. It's difficult to face the possibility that what you once trusted, and even taught, was not the full truth. Reconciling the Old and New Testaments eventually proved impossible for me.

Another challenge has been dealing with the reactions of others. Many of my peers in the church aren't ready to hear about the Seven Laws or to question their long-held interpretations of Scripture. I was especially shaken when I began to recognize the antisemitic threads woven into some New Testament teachings. Facing that reality was very uncomfortable, but also necessary.

These struggles taught me to walk with courage and humility in my faith journey, even when it meant walking a path that few around me were willing to take.

5. How has following this path changed your life?

My life has been enriched because of it. Understanding that the Noahide Laws are eternal and universal has given me a framework for life and has helped me embrace my role within humanity. Rabbi Singer explained that these commandments, given to Noah, are G-d's guidance for the Gentile world. That understanding lifted the internal conflict that had plagued me for years and replaced it with a sense of peace and direction.

Embracing the Seven Laws has also brought me into a community of like-minded individuals who are seeking truth and striving to live righteous lives. This path has made me a better listener and a more thoughtful person. I'm less focused on being "right" and more focused on understanding others and building meaningful connections. It's not just about learning and following laws; it's about living with purpose and reflecting G-d's guidance in how I treat others and approach the world.

6. What are you currently learning?

Right now, I'm digging into the Torah, but this time, I'm looking at it through a Noahide lens. It's like I'm reading it with a fresh view, focusing on the universal principles meant for all of humanity instead of trying to make everything fit into a Christian framework. It's been a real eye-opener.

I'm also learning how to talk about this in a way that people can actually hear it. I'm not out here trying to convert anyone, that's not the point. But if I can share the peace and clarity I've found, and maybe help someone else start asking their own questions, then that's what I want to do. At the same time, I'm learning to respect where people are in their journey. It's not my job to push them, just to share what I've learned and let them decide what to do with it.

7. How do you apply what you learn to your daily life?

Living by the Seven Laws is about trying to do the right thing every day. It's in the small stuff, being honest, showing kindness, treating people with respect. I think about the Laws in every decision I make, whether it's how I talk to someone, how I handle a problem, or how I show up in the world. It's not always easy, but it's always worth it.

I've also gotten more involved with the Noahide community. I go to Shabbat dinners and learn from rabbis and other Jewish leaders. It's so wonderful connecting with people who are on the same path. That connection has been life-changing for me.

And let me tell you, I'll never forget that shopkeeper in Israel. When I said I was "just" a Noahide, he looked at me like I'd said the dumbest thing he'd ever heard. I still hear him say, "Don't you ever say 'just'!" Now, every day, I remind myself to be proud of this path; it's a way of life that connects me to Hashem and gives me a purpose. I try to live it out in a way that makes others want to ask questions and maybe start their own journey. It's a work in progress, but it's the most meaningful thing I've ever done.

KEY LESSONS

1. **Questioning is the start of growth.** My journey began with doubts about the teachings of my childhood. My curiosity and willingness to seek answers led me to a path of clarity and purpose.

2. **Truth can come from unexpected places.** A casual conversation with my barber planted the seed that led me to discover the Noahide Laws. Wisdom often arrives when we least expect it.

3. **Clarity comes from understanding context.** Learning that G-d's Laws for Noah and Moses were meant for different audiences helped me reconcile years of religious conflict, showing me how understanding context can unlock deeper truths.

4. **Unlearning is as important as learning.** One of my biggest challenges was unlearning decades of deeply ingrained teachings. Sometimes, letting go of what no longer serves us is essential for growth.

5. **Humility and courage are essential for faith journeys.** Confronting uncomfortable truths, like the antisemitic interpretations I discovered in my past faith, required me to practice humility and courage, even when it meant walking a lonely path.

6. **Faith is about living, not just believing.** For me, embracing the Noahide Laws isn't about rituals; it's about living with purpose, treating others with kindness, and making ethical decisions in everyday life.

7. **Be proud of your path.** My encounter with the Israeli shopkeeper reminded me, and continues to remind me, not to diminish the importance of my spiritual choices. Every path has its purpose and value.

15.

Anne Marie Laseur | (Netherlands)

FROM QUESTIONS TO CLARITY

"Discovering the Seven Noahide Laws transformed my life, showing me that clarity, connection, and purpose come not from rigid boundaries, but from aligning with universal truths."

1. What is your background?

I was born in the Netherlands, on the Veluwe. My parents had recently returned from South Africa, where they had lived for twelve years. While they always retained a longing for South Africa, I felt a strong connection to the Netherlands. My parents were Protestant, and we attended the Reformed Church. I have fond memories of the dark church pews, candlelight, and the depth of the sermons, particularly those focusing on the Old Testament. These early experiences sparked my interest in the Hebrew language and Judaism.

I completed higher vocational education and have worked since then in mental health care, specifically in a psychiatric clinic. I am married and live in a small village. My childhood was marked by curiosity and a desire for depth, which eventually led to a broader search for faith and spirituality. My parents had a love-hate relationship with the church, being independent thinkers who later distanced themselves from organized religion. Despite this, I remained interested in spirituality. During my time in a student association, I encountered various denominations and discovered the beauty of connecting with others and learning how different believers and non-believers approach life. This personal quest for faith and depth eventually led to my interest in ecumenical mysticism and, later, Orthodox Judaism.

2. How did you discover the Seven Laws of Noah?

I came across the Seven Noahide Laws when Rabbi Perets, the founder of the Noahide Academy of Jerusalem, invited me through Facebook to attend a Noahide Conference. At the time, I knew very little about Noahide beliefs, but I felt strongly drawn to them and decided to travel to Jerusalem for the conference.

During the event, things started to fall into place. The historical and theological background was explained clearly, and for the first time I understood how the Noahide Laws create a bridge between Judaism and non-Jews. It gave me a much deeper understanding of my own spiritual path. I can honestly say it felt like a revelation: a solid tradition and foundation that allowed me to have a direct connection with G-d, without the Christian doctrines I had long struggled with.

3. What impact did this knowledge have on you?

It has had a deep impact on me. The lessons provided me with wisdom and structure, offering clarity about my position and helping me intellectually part ways with certain Christian doctrines. Emotionally, it was challenging at times. A few family members and friends could not understand my choice and broke off contact. However, this gave me the space to walk my own path.

Professionally and socially, this new perspective enriched my life. My work in mental health care, for example, has benefited from insights gained through the Noahide teachings. In daily life,

I began dedicating more time to study, prayer, and meditation. Rabbinic lessons provided depth and inspiration, and my growing passion for the Hebrew language helped me better understand foundational texts and concepts.

4. What has been your biggest challenge?

The biggest challenge has been the lack of physical connection with fellow believers. We are scattered across the Netherlands, and while we try to meet three or four times a year, it doesn't compare to the weekly gatherings I was used to.

Another challenge is the practical separation from Orthodox Judaism. While we are deeply connected to it, we don't fully integrate with it in a practical sense, which can feel isolating. We address this by attending Zoom gatherings and participating in Jewish festivals whenever possible.

Additionally, explaining the Noahide Laws to others is not always easy. People often misunderstand what it entails, sometimes seeing it as a strange sect or a Jewish variant of Christianity. Finding the right words and building bridges to explain this path has been a significant learning process.

Finally, balancing minimal and maximal interpretations of Noahide practice has been a challenge. Some argue that one should only follow the basic Seven Commandments, while others advocate for a more comprehensive practice, including structured prayer times and study. I've learned to find a middle ground and allow others the freedom to choose their approach. Personally, I embrace simplicity, with daily prayer, gratitude, meaningful activities, and helping others. On Saturday, I take extra time to study, recite Psalms aloud, and slow down, my way of acknowledging the seventh day.

This path has made me stronger, both spiritually and emotionally. It has provided a solid foundation and a sense of connection to an ancient tradition, helping me feel deeply connected to Hashem and my own essence.

5. How has following this path changed your life?

Following the Noahide path has profoundly transformed my life, shaping how I view relationships, community, and my sense of purpose. On a personal level, it has taught me to prioritize respect, compassion, and the recognition that every person is created in the Divine image. This perspective has deepened my relationships and helped me approach disagreements with greater patience, humility, and understanding.

The Noahide principles have led me to live with greater fairness and accountability. These values are not abstract ideals, but practical standards that guide my daily interactions and help build trust and integrity.

I work to spread awareness of the Seven Noahide Commandments and foster a supportive community. Through writing blog posts, translating Noahide books, and organizing events with guest speakers, I aim to reach and inspire as many people as possible. Sharing this perspective with others has been a meaningful way to connect and create positive change.

This path has also given me a renewed sense of purpose. Translating the Noahide principles into tangible actions, like promoting kindness and fairness, has allowed me to inspire curiosity about this way of life without imposing my beliefs on others.

The Seven Laws have also reshaped how I define success. Instead of measuring achievements solely by worldly standards, I now focus on how closely my actions align with Divine values. This perspective has brought a deep sense of peace and fulfillment, knowing that my efforts contribute to a greater purpose beyond myself.

6. What are you currently learning?

I am currently working with the leadership team of the Dutch Noahide Community on projects such as maintaining the website, organizing discussion groups, and coordinating lessons. We have also created an informational guide for beginning Noahides, with the goal of presenting the core principles of the Noahide Laws in a way that is clear and accessible.

Alongside this work, I continue to learn through podcasts, online lessons, and books. One important area of focus for me is understanding the teachings of different rabbis and learning how to navigate apparent contradictions between them. This ongoing study not only strengthens my own path, but also helps me support others in our community..

7. How do you apply what you learn to your daily life?

I apply my knowledge through prayer, meditation, and daily choices. If someone is ill, I pray for them. I often seek solitude to organize my thoughts and connect with Hashem. Jewish wisdom has offered valuable insights into psychology and personal development, which I incorporate into my work and relationships.

Practically, I've adopted more modest clothing and placed greater importance on dignity in how I present myself. I am more conscious of my choices, avoiding violent or superficial entertainment. These changes reflect my commitment to living in harmony with the Noahide Laws.

In my interactions, I strive to listen attentively, avoid gossip, treat animals well, and seek opportunities for connection, truth, and upliftment. Saturday, the seventh day, in particular, is a time for me to slow down, study, and express gratitude, aligning my life with Divine values.

KEY LESSONS

1. **Spiritual growth begins with curiosity and openness.** My early fascination with Judaism and spirituality led me to explore beyond the boundaries of my upbringing. Seeking depth in faith requires a willingness to question, learn, and grow, even when it means stepping outside of familiar traditions.

2. **Finding truth often requires letting go.** Embracing the Seven Noahide Laws meant intellectually and emotionally parting ways with certain Christian doctrines. It wasn't easy, especially when some friends and family couldn't understand my decision. But finding truth requires the courage to release what no longer aligns with one's convictions.

3. **Community matters, even when it's hard to find.** Being part of a scattered Noahide community in the Netherlands has been challenging, but I've learned to create connection in other ways. Whether through online gatherings, occasional in-person meetings, or shared learning, finding spiritual support, even at a distance, has been essential.

4. **Living with purpose means applying wisdom to everyday life.** My work in mental health care has been enriched by the ethical insights I've gained from Noahide teachings. The wisdom of the Torah isn't just about study, it's about applying Divine principles in how I treat others, make decisions, and conduct myself with integrity.

5. **Balance is key in religious practice.** Navigating different interpretations of Noahide observance has taught me that there is no single "right" way to follow this path. I've learned to embrace simplicity, prayer, study, gratitude, and acts of kindness, while allowing others the freedom to approach their practice in a way that speaks to them.

6. **Spreading awareness creates meaningful connections.** Translating Noahide texts, writing blogs, and organizing events has given me a sense of mission. Sharing this wisdom with others not only strengthens my own understanding but helps build a more informed and connected Noahide community.

7. **Faith is a journey of continuous learning.** Whether through personal study, rabbinic teachings, or discussions within the Noahide community, I am always deepening my understanding. Learning Torah and integrating its wisdom into my daily life has given me clarity, fulfillment, and a greater sense of responsibility in my spiritual journey.

16.

Eliyahu Greenwald | (Israel)

A LIFE REWRITTEN

"The search for meaning often leads through fire,
but Hashem always provides a way home."

1. What is your background?

I was raised in a nominal Christian environment. My first experience in a church was terrifying, I walked in and saw a crucifix with Jesus hanging there, bleeding. I was so scared I refused to go inside. My mother wanted me to go with some nuns on a tour with my siblings and other family members, but I threw a fit and refused. My mom and stepdad were furious, but I just couldn't go in.

Six months later, we went to church again, maybe for Easter or Christmas, and I started asking other kids who the man on the cross was. They told me, "Oh, that's Jesus. Don't worry about him; he ain't gonna hurt you." And that was that. I continued living a very nominal Christian life. I attended church sporadically as a child, but never felt deeply connected to it.

Then, at sixteen, I was told about my real father, who was Jewish. That revelation completely upended my sense of identity, not just emotionally, but psychologically. I had grown up thinking I was Jim Shade. But suddenly, I learned my real last name was Greenwald. I had been born James David Greenwald, but raised as James David Shade after my parents divorced when I was three. Finding out the truth left me feeling lost. Who was I? My mother and stepfather painted my father in the worst possible light; someone to fear, despise, and forget. That version of him left no room for love, no space for questions. That was the narrative I was given.

I had no idea why they had waited until I was sixteen to tell me, but there I was, suddenly questioning everything. I became curious about Judaism and started reading books from the library, but I didn't go much deeper at that point. I was busy running around, being a kid. Then we moved to Arizona, and things took a darker turn.

After moving, I got into trouble with the law, stealing, drinking, and getting caught with stolen goods. I ended up in a juvenile institution. And that's where I first encountered Islam.

2. How did you discover the Seven Laws of Noah?

During my time in the institution, I was surrounded by people of various religious backgrounds: many were Muslim, some were Christian, and I even met a couple of Hindus. At that time in my life, I was searching for something, though I didn't quite know what.

I began studying Islam and became deeply involved in it. I was drawn to its structure and sense of belonging, but I eventually found myself in a group that focused on an extreme and radical interpretation. The ideology emphasized hostility toward those outside the faith, and I was pushed to prove my loyalty in ways that made me deeply uncomfortable.

One day, I was out with the group, and they pressured me to act violently toward someone simply because of their religious identity. That was the moment I realized I was heading down a dangerous path. Instead of complying, I walked away, and then I ran. Because in that world, hesitation or defiance could be met with severe consequences.

That experience was a turning point. I started questioning everything I had been immersed in and began exploring other religions. I delved into Buddhism and Hinduism, but neither provided the clarity I was looking for. I then turned to Christianity, attending a fervent church community, but again, something felt off. It was more about fitting in than truly connecting with the faith.

At one point, I even became involved with a group that framed itself as a Christian movement but functioned more like a militant organization. Over time, I realized that many of these groups, despite their differences, operated with a similar mentality of exclusion and opposition. When I stepped away, I found myself isolated once again.

Later, I was introduced to Messianic Judaism and the Seventh-day Adventist movement, but my questions remained. It wasn't until I attended a Passover *seder* in Phoenix, Arizona, that I felt something different. Walking into that synagogue, immersed in the traditions of Passover, I experienced a profound sense of belonging.

While in Austin, Texas, I met Hasidic Jews who introduced me to the concept of the Noahide Laws. At the time, I set it aside, but years later, I revisited the idea. This time, I studied it seriously, and for the first time in my long search, I found a framework that resonated with me deeply.

3. What impact did this knowledge have on you?

When I retired at sixty-five, I decided to devote myself to study. At first, I thought about converting to Judaism. I even moved to Israel with that goal. I lived in the West Bank, surrounded by Palestinian towns, hearing gunfire constantly. I studied for over a year and a half, diving deep into Torah, Jewish law, and Jewish philosophy. But ultimately, I realized I couldn't take on the full responsibility of Jewish *mitzvot*. The enormity of it weighed on me, I questioned whether I could truly commit to such a life.

One day, during deep prayer, I heard Hashem's voice tell me: "Be a Noahide." That was when I finally understood my path. It wasn't about converting; it was about embodying the universal ethics Hashem had given to all humanity.

4. What has been your biggest challenge?

Losing my identity, being raised with antisemitic beliefs despite my Jewish roots, homelessness at seventy, these were all major struggles. Choosing to be a Noahide instead of converting was another. Walking away from the familiarity of religious institutions and carving out my own relationship with Hashem required deep faith and conviction. It meant forging a new identity outside of rigid religious labels. It meant enduring loneliness at times, as I no longer fit neatly into any religious group. It meant navigating the misconceptions others had about Noahides; many people don't understand the depth of our commitment to Hashem. Even within Jewish communities, acceptance wasn't always immediate. But through it all, I held firm to my decision, knowing that this path was the right one for me.

5. How has following this path changed your life?

I no longer chase miracles. I have complete faith in Hashem. I live in Israel, surrounded by religious Jews who respect my decision. My faith is stronger than it has ever been. Every day, I wake up with a sense of purpose and peace, knowing I am fulfilling my role in the world. I have found a deep sense of belonging, even without formal conversion. The wisdom of the Torah guides my daily choices, and I take comfort in knowing that I am walking the path Hashem intended for me. The more I study and live by the Seven Laws, the more clarity and joy I experience. My life is no longer about seeking external validation, my relationship with Hashem is enough.

6. What are you currently learning?

I study Torah and the Seven Noahide Laws daily, focusing on ethical monotheism and living a righteous life as a non-Jew. My studies encompass classical Jewish texts, including the works of Rambam and *the Talmud*[44], to understand the foundational ethics of Noahide life. My learning isn't just theoretical. I apply it to my daily interactions, striving to improve my character, practice gratitude, and uphold justice. Additionally, I explore the historical context of the Noahide Laws, examining their significance across civilizations and their relevance today. I also study Hebrew to enhance my comprehension of sacred texts and prayers. Each day is a journey of refinement, aligning my actions more closely with Hashem's will.

7. How do you apply what you learn to your daily life?

I strive to live by the *Shema*[45], hearing and doing with intention.

I take a hands-on approach to improving my community. Riding around town on my scooter, I make it a priority to pick up trash and fix small things in need of repair, ensuring a cleaner and more functional environment. Recently, children in the community created a beautiful artwork to express their gratitude for my efforts. Their gesture was a touching reminder of how even the smallest acts of care can inspire others and foster a sense of unity.

---

44. See Additional Information on pg. 199.

45. *Shema* is the first word in Hebrew of the verse Deuteronomy 6:4.

My philosophy is simple: follow Hashem, and everything else will fall into place. The more I dedicate myself to living a life of righteousness, the more I see its positive impact, both in my personal fulfillment and in the lives of those around me.

KEY LESSONS

1. **Identity is not given, it's discovered.** Learning my Jewish heritage on my father's side at sixteen shattered everything I thought I knew about myself. Until then, I lived under a different last name and a false story. Discovering my birth name, Greenwald, forced me to question who I really was. That moment launched me on a long journey to find my true identity, not the one shaped by others. Identity is something we must seek through truth, not something handed to us.

2. **Blind faith is dangerous, but true faith is liberating.** My search led me through Christianity, Islam, and Messianic movements. But when I got caught in religious extremism, I saw how blind faith without wisdom leads to destruction. Being pressured to commit violence in the name of religion taught me that faith must be rooted in truth and righteousness. Only when I found the Noahide Laws did I experience faith that uplifts and liberates.

3. **Running away can be the first step toward running home.** I had to walk away from people demanding violent loyalty. Leaving behind Islam, Christianity, and other false paths felt like failure, but it was really the start of finding Hashem. Sometimes running from what's wrong is how we start running toward what's right. That's how I discovered my role as a Noahide.

4. **A meaningful life is not about labels, but about righteousness.** For years, I considered converting to Judaism. I even moved to Israel and studied Torah and Jewish law. But through prayer, I came to understand that my path was not about taking on a label, but about living as Hashem intended for me. Following the Seven Laws and striving to act with integrity gave my life genuine meaning.

5. **Every action matters, no matter how small.** Today, I ride my scooter around town, picking up trash and fixing small things others ignore. These simple acts make a real difference. Righteousness is about daily choices to do good.

6. **The past does not define me, but it shapes my wisdom.** I've faced struggles; being raised with antisemitic beliefs, getting into legal trouble, battling cancer, and experiencing homelessness. These painful experiences shaped me. They taught me resilience, compassion, and humility. My past doesn't define me, but it has made me wiser and more committed to living with integrity.

7. **Hashem's voice is the only one I need to follow.** There are many loud voices, religious leaders, communities, family, but I've learned to listen to Hashem. In deep prayer, I heard Him say, "*Be a Noahide.*" Since then, that's been my guide. Following Hashem's will gives me peace and purpose.

17.

Nancy Grooms | (USA)

CHARTING THE UNKNOWN

"Once I encountered the truth of the one G-d, there was no turning back. The path wasn't easy, but the depth and beauty I've found make every step worthwhile."

1. What is your background?

I was raised in a Christian home, but my parents died when I was only eleven years old. After that, I lived with different families, first with relatives and later in foster homes. It was a difficult period, and during those years I was exposed to several different Christian denominations.

At eighteen, while still in high school, I moved out and started living on my own. A year later, I got married and became Catholic. Over the years, through life and marriage, I was also involved in Evangelicalism and other expressions of Christianity. Church life had always been a central part of my upbringing. As a child, I attended children's church, sometimes helped lead lessons, and was involved in outreach projects where I mentored younger children and helped others.

The Catholic Church felt different to me. It seemed closer to Judaism in its reverence, structure, and sense of sacredness. Even though I knew it was not fully right for me, I did appreciate the seriousness and holiness it conveyed.

My journey has been one of searching, questioning, and trying to find something deeper and more true.

2. How did you discover the Seven Laws of Noah?

In my 40s, I reached a turning point. After years of navigating difficult marriages and exploring different Christian traditions, I finally told G-d, "I don't want to hear about You from others anymore. I want You to teach me directly."

Shortly after, I stumbled across a poster in my small town advertising a weekend seminar. The speaker, someone with a Jewish perspective, was talking about the End Times[46]. I felt compelled to go. By the end of the weekend, I left behind Christian holidays and traditions, like Christmas and Easter, and started learning about the Jewish calendar and G-d's appointed times.

The seminar itself came out of a Messianic Jewish setting, and at that stage I did not yet understand the difference between that and traditional Judaism. Over the next several years, through learning, asking questions, and finding the right mentors, I gradually came to understand and embrace the Noahide path more fully. Teachers such as Jeremy Gimpel, Ari Abramowitz, and Moshe Kempinski played an important role in guiding me along the way.

3. What impact did this knowledge have on you?

Discovering the Seven Laws of Noah has been the greatest and most profound gift I've ever received, knowing the one true G-d and understanding His truth. There's nothing greater.

Learning about the Seven Laws opened up a path of endless growth and study. Unlike in Christianity, where the teachings felt

---

46. This is the Jewish expression for the period of world history just before the beginning of the Messianic Era.

limited, this new path provided an infinite depth of wisdom to explore. Every teaching resonated with me as truth, and I knew I could never turn back.

4. What has been your biggest challenge?

At the beginning, the greatest challenge was the isolation. I live in a small town of about 10,000 people, and everyone knew us. When I started following the Noahide path, people thought I had joined a cult. Even my brother considered having me investigated. My kids were ostracized at school, and it felt like the community had turned on us.

Over time, that initial resistance faded, but the challenges I face today are more personal. I now focus on refining my character, growing spiritually, and trying to be a light to others. It is a daily effort to stay focused on truth and to live with purpose.

5. How has following this path changed your life?

The Noahide path has completely changed my life. It has given me clarity, and a strong connection to G-d. Honoring the seventh day has become one of the most transformative aspects of our lives. At first, it was a major adjustment, shifting from a typical Saturday filled with errands and projects to a day of some rest and reflection. Now, my family and I look forward to it every week.

This journey has also strengthened my family. My oldest son, after exploring on his own, embraced the path and is now raising his children as Noahides. My youngest son and his wife are deeply committed as well. Even though my daughter faces challenges with a husband who doesn't share her beliefs, she continues to practice on her own.

6. What are you currently learning?

I'm currently studying *Tomer Devorah*[47] and delving deeper into the *Tanya*[48]. These texts give incredible insights into refining one's character and drawing closer to G-d. I also follow weekly teachings on the Torah portion from Rabbi Chaim Richman and participate in the Land of Israel Fellowship, led by Rabbi Jeremy Gimpel and Rabbi Ari Abramowitz.

Every day brings an opportunity to learn something new, whether it's through structured study or simply reflecting on G-d's teachings in my life.

7. How do you apply what you learn to your daily life?

I try to bring what I've learned into my everyday interactions. At work, when I deal with customers who are upset or stressed, I remind myself to stay calm and be a steady, positive presence. I try to respond with humility, patience, and kindness, guided by teachings that stress self-restraint and letting go of my own ego.

Each day is an opportunity to grow closer to G-d, to work on myself, and to deepen my understanding of His truth. Whether it's honoring the seventh day, practicing gratitude, or studying Torah, my goal is to live a life that reflects the wisdom of this path.

---

47. *Tomer Devorah (The Palm Tree of Deborah)*, written in the 16th century by Rabbi Moshe Cordovero of Safed, is an ethical and Kabbalistic guide to emulating G-d's 13 Attributes of Mercy (hinted to in Michah 7:18-20) as a path to personal refinement.

48. See Additional Information on pg. 199.

KEY LESSONS

1. **Trust the journey.** There were times when I felt isolated, and misunderstood. But I learned to trust that every step forward was guided by G-d. Even in the hardest moments, I knew I couldn't turn back, truth is worth any challenge.

2. **Growth is unlimited.** Unlike the religious teachings I had known before, which often felt limiting, the wisdom of the Torah offers endless depth. Every time I study, I uncover new insights that refine my understanding and help me grow into the person G-d wants me to be.

3. **Community matters.** At first, I felt completely alone, judged by those around me and even questioned by my own family. Over time, I found teachers, mentors, and a global community that gave me support and strength. Even in isolation, having others to learn from and connect with has been life-changing.

4. **The seventh day transforms.** The seventh day was one of the biggest adjustments in my journey, but it quickly became one of the most meaningful parts of my life. Taking a day to pause, reflect, and connect with G-d has brought a sense of peace and purpose to my life.

5. **Apply what you learn.** It's not enough to study wisdom, you have to live it. I work on bringing patience, humility, and kindness into my everyday interactions, whether with my family, my community, or even difficult customers at work. Every challenge is an opportunity to put spiritual teachings into practice.

6. **Challenges build strength.** My journey hasn't been easy, but every struggle has shaped me. From facing criticism to overcoming personal doubts, I've learned that resilience comes from staying committed to truth, no matter the obstacles. Growth is about what you gain and what you overcome.

7. **Faith is a daily practice.** I connect to G-d through small, daily acts. Studying Torah, practicing gratitude, refining my character, and striving to be a light to others; these are the ways I bring faith into every aspect of my life.

18.

Craig Lodice | (USA)

FINDING G-D WITHOUT CONVERTING

"Raised without religion and rejected for my beliefs, I discovered purpose in a path most people have never heard of."

1. What is your background?

I was born in Helena, Arkansas, just south of Memphis, Tennessee. My mom's marriage to a man named Charles ended not long after I was born. Later she met Tom Lodice, the man who adopted me, gave me his name, and raised me as his own. I've never met my biological father. A lot of who I am comes from the fact that Tom chose to raise me as his son. He was from Rochester, New York, so we spent a good amount of time visiting up there. That mix gave me both Southern roots and a little bit of New York grit.

My parents were basically hippies, not religious, but not hostile to religion either. My dad had a Catholic background. My mom didn't really have any religious upbringing. I wasn't raised to believe anything in particular, and now I consider that a blessing. I had room to think freely, ask questions, and follow the truth without feeling like I was betraying something I inherited.

Even as a little kid, I had questions. I remember being around six or seven when my mom bought me this pair of sandals. I hated them. I was probably making a big scene about it when my dad looked at me and said, "What's the big deal? Jesus wore sandals." I wrinkled my nose and asked, "Who's that guy?" Just deadpan, no clue. That moment says a lot about how I was raised. There was no pressure to know who Jesus was, no bedtime Bible stories. I had a blank slate. And because of that, I wasn't locked into anything. When I started asking bigger questions later in life, I didn't have to fight my way out of anything. I could just walk away when things didn't make sense.

I started going to church on my own when I was around eight years old. It wasn't about faith at first; my friends went, so I went. Eventually I started attending an Episcopal church in Helena, St. John's. It was beautiful, and the people were kind. Around age thirteen, I started taking it seriously. I even broke down crying once, telling the priest I didn't understand G-d. He came to visit my family afterward. My parents were supportive, they thought it was great that I was searching for meaning and going to church instead of getting into trouble.

2. How did you discover the Seven Laws of Noah?

In 1995, I signed up for a speech class in high school, expecting to learn how to give public speeches. Instead, our teacher, Stephanie Graznik, spent the entire semester teaching us about the Holocaust. She didn't just present dry history, she showed us the propaganda, the brainwashing, and how entire communities were led to believe Jews were subhuman. That shook me.

I started seeing how religious language had been twisted throughout history to justify horrific acts. In many of the photos and newsreels we studied, high-ranking Nazis were standing in churches, or using Christian references in speeches. It hit me hard that many of those involved in the machinery of genocide came from Christian backgrounds, people who had grown up hearing sermons on Sunday and yet participated in mass murder during the week. That contradiction haunted me. I couldn't make peace with it.

It was around that time that I began pulling away from church. I had gone faithfully for years, but this new understanding made it impossible to keep sitting in the pews like nothing had changed. I started asking deeper questions, about history, G-d, and what it really meant to live a moral life.

Then, in 2000, I walked into a Barnes & Noble and picked up a copy of *Judaism for Dummies*. I opened to a page about Hashem being the One Creator of the universe. That language hit me like a lightning bolt. I had never heard G-d described that way in church. It felt ancient, unchanging, and true.

I started studying Judaism seriously. I even tried to convert. I visited both Reform and Orthodox synagogues, but ultimately gravitated toward the Orthodox community. They seemed grounded, like they were trying to preserve something sacred instead of reshaping it to fit the times.

Eventually I went to Young Israel of Memphis and spoke to Rabbi Yoda Silver. He turned me down for conversion, but in that conversation, he introduced me to the Seven Noahide Laws. Later I was referred to Rabbi Malevsky, who gave me a copy of *The Path of the Righteous Gentile*[49] and connected me with a Noahide named Roy Grissom. Roy and I began learning together, and that's when I realized there was a real, meaningful, and Divinely guided path for Gentiles, a path I hadn't known even existed.

---

49. The authorized 1987 edition, titled *The Path of the Righteous Gentile: An Introduction to the Seven Laws of the Children of Noah.*

3. What impact did this knowledge have on you?

Everything changed, my whole life changed. Suddenly I had direction, and structure. I started shaping my life around *The Divine Code,* which became my main source of study. The Seven Laws weren't just ideas, they were a way of life.

I began raising my children with those values. We talked about morality in daily life. I remember learning in *The Divine Code* that downloading music without paying for it was considered theft. That hit me. I had done that before without even thinking about it. Realizing that even that mattered taught me how serious Hashem's Laws are, and how they apply in real life.

I named some of my children after Biblical Jewish heroes. We played *Hatikvah*[50] in the house, discussed Jewish values, and made Israel a part of our family's story. I may not be Jewish, but I found a spiritual home in the Seven Laws.

4. What has been your biggest challenge?

Without question, being alone.

I live in Canyon, Texas. The nearest Orthodox synagogue is four to six hours away. Most people around me have never even heard of the Seven Laws of Noah. If they have, they assume it's a cult or that I've lost my mind.

When I stopped going to church, my family turned on me. I went from being the pride of the family to being the one they whispered about. I've had teachers try to convert my kids at school. I've had Children Protective Services (CPS) call on me for not taking my children to church. The social pressure has been crushing at times.

---

50. The title of the national anthem of the State of Israel.

But I've stayed the course. I've kept studying, kept raising my kids with these values, and kept reaching out to people like Dr. Michael Schulman and Rabbi Moshe Weiner who've helped guide me along the way.

5. How has following this path changed your life?

Following these Laws has removed a spiritual burden I didn't even realize I was carrying. I'm not just reacting to life anymore, I'm aligned with something eternal. I know what to do when I mess up. I know how to live in a way that honors my Creator.

I've also seen the ripple effects. I've watched my kids ask better questions. I've seen how they think through ethical choices. I've seen people change just by watching how we live. That makes the hard parts worth it.

6. What are you currently learning?

I'm going deeper into *The Divine Code* again. I've been doing this for a long time, but there's always more to learn. I see *The Divine Code* as the Gentile version of the Talmud; it's how we know which parts of the Torah apply to us and which don't.

If I have a question, I go to Dr. Schulman or Rabbi Weiner. Their knowledge is thorough, rooted in real sources, and deeply trustworthy. I also keep up with Israel through news and media. I want my kids to grow up knowing that this path is connected to something much bigger than us.

7. How do you apply what you learn to your daily life?

Everything goes through the filter of the Seven Laws. When one of my kids takes something that's not theirs, we talk about the Torah laws against theft. When they hear something at school that contradicts our values, we sit down and work through it.

I don't always manage formal study sessions with my kids, because life is busy. But I live the values. And I answer their questions. I point them to the right resources. A few of them have even spoken directly with Dr. Schulman when they had deep questions. This is not just theory for us. It's how we live.

KEY LESSONS

1. **I was never boxed in by dogma, and that gave me room to seek truth.** Growing up without religious pressure meant I could question things freely. That ability to ask hard questions, without fear, opened the door to everything I've learned since.

2. **When I saw the truth, I couldn't unsee it.** The Holocaust education I received shattered any illusion I had about the moral infallibility of Christianity. Once I saw that, I couldn't return to blind faith. That moment set me on a new path.

3. ***The Divine Code* taught me what real integrity looks like.** I didn't realize downloading music was theft until I read about property laws in *The Divine Code*. That was humbling. Now I weigh even the smallest actions against what Hashem expects of me.

4. **This path has cost me relationships, but it gave me purpose.** I've been misunderstood, mocked, and rejected even by my own family. But I wouldn't trade the sense of peace and purpose I've gained for their approval.

5. **I don't just teach my kids, I live it with them.** I've taught my kids not through lectures, but through life. When they mess up, we talk. When they ask questions, we find answers. My home is my classroom, and I try to be the kind of man they'll want to learn from.

6. **Peace comes from knowing where you stand, not from comfort.** Even when life is hard, I don't feel aimless. I know Hashem is with me. That sense of spiritual security gets me through the hardest days.

7. **I'm not a Jew, but I have a holy mission.** I may not have a Jewish soul, but I have a Noahide purpose. I'm here to serve Hashem with the tools I've been given. I'm building something real, not just for myself, but for my children and generations to come.

19.

Jennifer Woodward | (USA)

A PATH ROOTED IN CONNECTION AND GROWTH

"Even when I don't understand the purpose of something, I trust that it's there. That belief keeps me grounded, and gives me peace."

1. What is your background?

I grew up in a non-denominational Christian family, where faith was always present, though not in a rigid or highly structured way. It was more about personal belief and connecting with G-d on an individual level rather than adhering to a formal doctrine. Over the years, my mom and I would attend an outdoor church in Ashland, Oregon, off and on. These gatherings were unique; they took place in a park, surrounded by nature, with the sky above us. Being outdoors gave the experience a sense of freedom and connection to the Creator in a way that felt very different from traditional indoor church services.

The outdoor church gatherings weren't something we attended every week, but they did become a meaningful touchpoint in our spiritual lives. They helped foster a love for community and a sense of openness in exploring faith.

Later in life, I became curious about the Hebrew roots of Christianity. This curiosity led me to attend gatherings that emphasized deeper study of scripture and an interactive approach to worship. These gatherings were lively, full of dancing, tambourines, flags, and potlucks. There was an emphasis on community, and we even studied Hebrew together. Learning Hebrew opened my eyes to new perspectives on scripture and brought a richer dimension to my faith.

These experiences were all about connection with others, with the Creator, and with myself. Over time, the group dissolved, and people went in different directions. Some returned to traditional Christianity, others pursued Judaism, and some, like me, began exploring the Seven Noahide Laws.

2. How did you discover the Seven Laws of Noah?

My discovery of the Seven Noahide Laws was the result of years of searching and questioning. After exploring the Hebrew roots of Christianity, I still felt I was looking for more, a framework that was not confined to one religion but spoke to a universal truth.

That search led me to the Noahide Laws. At first, I encountered them through reading and study. What struck me was how clear and practical they were. They offered a way to live a righteous life that felt relevant to all people, not just as laws, but as ethical guidance.

As I dug deeper, I realized these Laws gave me exactly what I had been looking for. They offered a way to honor the Creator and live a meaningful life without needing to convert to Judaism. That felt freeing, because it was not about rejecting my past or denying where I came from.

The more I studied, the more these principles resonated with me. They became a framework for how I approached everything: family, work, relationships, and even the challenges that come with being human. The Noahide Laws became not just something I believed in, but something I lived by.

3. What impact did this knowledge have on you?

The knowledge of the Seven Noahide Laws has been transformative. It's like having a compass that guides me through life, no matter what's happening around me.

I've faced plenty of personal challenges over the years. One of the hardest was my struggle to conceive. Those years were filled with uncertainty, frustration, and moments of doubt. It was a difficult and emotional time. But through it all, my connection with the Creator helped me persevere. I held onto the belief that the Creator had a plan for me, even if I couldn't see it at the time. That trust became my anchor. And when I was finally blessed with children, I saw the fulfillment of that plan in ways I could never have imagined, and my trust in it was deepened.

This knowledge has also changed the way I approach everyday stress. Life can be unpredictable and chaotic, but the principles I've learned help me stay grounded. Instead of reacting with anxiety or frustration, I try to remind myself that there's a purpose to everything, even if it's not immediately clear.

4. What has been your biggest challenge?

One of my greatest challenges has been consistency. I've tried to incorporate practices like lighting candles on Friday nights or having a special meal to mark the seventh day. When I do these things, they feel meaningful and grounding. But life is busy, and there are times when I let these things slip away.

Another challenge is the sense of isolation I sometimes feel. There isn't a local Torah observant community near. The closest synagogue is in Ashland, but it's not practical for me to attend regularly. As a result, much of my spiritual journey has been solitary. I've relied on online communities and personal study to fill the gaps, but it's not the same as having a local group to share this path with.

Despite these challenges, I've learned to embrace the ebb and flow of life. Even when I'm not consistent in my practices, I try to focus on the bigger picture, my relationship with the Creator and the principles that guide me.

5. How has following this path changed your life?

This path has given me a sense of purpose and clarity that influences everything I do. It's about living in alignment with the Creator's will and seeing the beauty in every moment.

One of the biggest changes has been in how I approach challenges. Instead of seeing them as obstacles, I try to view them as opportunities for growth. This perspective shift has been profound. For example, during my struggles with pregnancy, I leaned on this belief to get through the hardest days. Now, as a mother, I see those challenges as part of a larger plan that brought me to where I am today.

This path has also transformed my relationships, especially with my family. My husband and I have a strong connection, and the peace I've found through this path has created a ripple effect in our home. I've learned that the energy I bring into our home has a powerful impact on those around me. If I'm calm and centered, it creates a peaceful atmosphere that benefits everyone else and helps them to do the same. But if I'm stressed or anxious, that energy spreads just as quickly.

6. What are you currently learning?

Right now, I'm diving into several texts that are challenging me to think deeply and grow spiritually. One of them is *Sha'ar HaKavanos*[51]. It's a dense and intricate work that requires slow, careful study. I can only take it a page at a time, but even that feels rewarding.

I'm also reading *The Spiritual Revolution of Rav Kook*, which has been on my list for years. His insights are profound and inspiring, and I'm finding so much wisdom in his writings. Additionally, I've started *Duties of the Heart*, a book that's helping me explore themes of gratitude, trust, and devotion. These texts are not easy reads, but they're worth the effort. Each one offers something unique, and together they're shaping how I view my relationship with the Creator and my place in the world.

7. How do you apply what you learn to your daily life?

Applying what I'm learning to daily life is a process of integration. I don't have a rigid schedule for study, I let inspiration guide me. My desk is piled with books, and there are bookshelves throughout my home. Whenever I have a few spare minutes, I try to pick up a book instead of my phone. Even reading just one page feels like progress.

I've also been focusing on building a more tangible relationship with the Creator. Recently, I started leaning more into Kabbalistic texts. These teachings have helped me see the Creator not as distant or abstract but as present in every moment.

---

51. *Sha'ar HaKavanos (Gate of Spiritual Meditations)*, authored by Rabbi Chaim Vital, is based on the teachings of his master, the Arizal (Rabbi Isaac Luria, 1534–1572). It records Lurianic kabbalistic intentions and practices associated with Jewish prayer, the Jewish Shabbat, and the Jewish festivals.

This shift has changed how I approach prayer and spirituality. Instead of only turning to the Creator in times of need, I try to live in a constant state of connection. I see the Creator's hand in everything, in every challenge, every joy, every ordinary moment. This mindset brings peace and purpose to my daily life.

KEY LESSONS

1. **Faith is a lifelong journey.** My spiritual path has been shaped by experiences that I never expected. From attending outdoor church services in Ashland as a child to studying Hebrew and exploring the Seven Noahide Laws, my understanding of faith has grown and deepened over time. Each step, even the confusing or difficult ones, has been part of a greater journey of connection with the Creator.

2. **Community shapes perspective.** Each of the groups I've been part of, whether the outdoor church, the Hebrew study group, or the Messianic community, played a role in my faith journey. Even when those communities dissolved or changed, they left a lasting impact. The friendships, the discussions, and the shared pursuit of truth helped shape the person I am today.

3. **Trust in the Creator's plan.** My struggles with pregnancy were one of the hardest tests of my faith. During those years of uncertainty and waiting, I had to learn to trust that the Creator had a plan, even when I couldn't see it. Now, looking at my children, I see the fulfillment of that plan in ways I never could have imagined at the time.

4. **Consistency is a challenge worth embracing.** I've tried to incorporate small spiritual practices into my life, like lighting candles on Friday night or setting aside time for study. Some weeks I do it, some weeks I don't. It's easy to feel like I'm not doing enough, but I've learned that faith isn't about perfection, it's about showing up in whatever way I can and keeping that connection alive.

5. **Learning deepens connection.** Studying Hebrew opened my eyes to new layers of meaning in the scriptures, and reading books like *Sha'ar HaKavanos* and *The Spiritual Revolution of Rav Kook* continues to challenge and inspire me. Learning isn't just an intellectual pursuit; it's a way of drawing closer to the Creator and discovering deeper truths about my own life.

6. **Peace starts within.** I've seen firsthand how the energy I bring into my home affects my family. When I'm centered and at peace, my husband and children feel it too. But when I'm anxious or overwhelmed, that energy spreads just as quickly. Learning to stay grounded in faith has helped me create a more peaceful and loving home environment.

7. **Every moment is an opportunity for growth.** Whether it's through study, personal challenges, or just noticing the Creator's presence in everyday life, I try to approach each day as an opportunity to grow. My journey hasn't been a straight path, but every experience, good or bad, has brought me closer to understanding my purpose and deepening my relationship with the Divine.

20.

Leba bat Noah | (USA)

A SEEKER'S JOURNEY

"The words of Genesis didn't just enter my mind, they woke up my soul."

1. What is your background?

I have always been a seeker. I knew there was "more between heaven and earth," but I never found a connection through the faith of my upbringing. I was raised in a nominally Christian home in the Netherlands. Both of my parents came from Catholic families. My father, of blessed memory, as the eldest son, was sent to seminary to become a priest. He left just before ordination, walked away from religion, and turned instead to philosophy.

When my parents got married and had children, they had us baptized, perhaps as a leftover from their own upbringing, but faith was not a central part of our home. Because we moved often, my sister and I went to whichever school was nearby, whether Catholic, Protestant, or public. I absorbed fragments from different traditions without ever really feeling to belong to any of them.

In the early 1980s, my father traveled to India for work and interviewed the Dalai Lama. That meeting made a deep impression on him. When he returned, he fully embraced Tibetan Buddhism and became a passionate supporter of the Tibetan cause. His enthusiasm woke up my own curiosity, and I began studying Tibetan Buddhism as well.

Later, while my father was taking classes in Tibetan language at a spiritual center in Amsterdam, I was there as well, studying Aikido and Shiatsu. Through that, I became interested in Zen Buddhism. From there, my search widened into earth-based spirituality, Wicca, and any path that seemed to offer answers. I was always looking for a way to connect to something higher, whatever that might be. Eventually, I was drawn to *alchemical fire circles,* sacred gatherings centered on inner psychological transformation.

That path brought me to the United States, where I met my first husband at *Fire Dance*, a sacred fire circle retreat in the Santa Cruz Mountains in California. After two years of long-distance dating we married, and I relocated. My first five years in the U.S. were a time of exploration: festivals, artistic communities, yoga, ecstatic dance, silent meditation retreats, and many spiritual gatherings. For a time, I was part of a Hindu *sangha* and studied under a guru.

Eventually, my first marriage ended. Not long after, I met the man who is now my husband.

2. How did you discover the Seven Laws of Noah?

A few months before the Covid pandemic began, my husband reached for a *Chumash,* the Five Books of Moses, from one of our many bookshelves and started reading aloud from *Bereishit,* the Book of Genesis. It seemed like a random moment, but as I listened it really grabbed me. The words actually *touched* me. I remember feeling excited and thinking, *"Does anyone else know how amazing these stories are?!"*

I had heard them as a child. We had a children's Bible with colorful illustrations, and I remember stories about Jonah and the Whale, and about Abraham and Sarah. I loved the pictures but the stories never did anything for me. This time it was different. What stood out was not only the text but the commentary woven through it. Until then I thought of the Bible as simply a collection of dusty old tales. The commentary revealed depth and meaning for daily life. It brought the words *alive.* Stories I once pooh-poohed now somehow spoke directly to me.

That same night, I went online in search of Torah study opportunities and found a class with our local Chabad Rabbi. Soon after, the pandemic arrived and the world screeched to a halt.

During that pause, when we were all in lockdown, something very special began for us. While so many people were suffering, my husband and I felt deeply grateful to have that time together. We spent hours reading, studying, and talking about Torah.

Then one afternoon, YouTube led me to a video about the Dutch Noahide Community. I had never heard the word "Noahide" before. The idea that non-Jews could study Torah felt exciting to me. It opened a door, and I knew I had found my place.

3. What impact did this knowledge have on you?

Throughout the lockdowns, Torah study became my anchor, my ark. It gave me structure and clarity during a difficult and confusing time. While many people felt trapped, I found a sense of freedom in the timeless wisdom of Torah.

This journey has also deepened my relationship with my husband. Torah became the language of our home, guiding how we treat one another. Judaism places relationships at the core of its teachings, and learning together helped us grow closer. Even now, beyond the pandemic, this path continues to shape me. I feel more mindful, more attuned to purpose, and more focused on serving others. It really has changed the way I live and do relationships.

I have also become much more aware of antisemitism in this world. The events of October 7, 2023, and the way Israel and the Jewish people have been portrayed in the media has left a deep impression on me. It has been staggering to witness the dark and destructive narrative that has taken hold. In the media, the portrayal seems to grow more hostile and disturbing with each passing day. I had already felt a strong connection to Israel and the Jewish people before these events, but afterward that connection has only consolidated and deepened.

4. What has been your biggest challenge?

I am blessed to have a strong Jewish community in my town. Being part of Chabad gives me the chance to learn, celebrate, and grow in a warm and welcoming environment. Many Noahides face isolation or struggle with relationships when their partners do not share their beliefs. I do not face those challenges.

The biggest challenge for me is simply wishing I had more time to learn. There is so much wisdom, and so many books I want to read. (So many books, so little time!) But I see this as a good challenge, because it means there is always more to explore.

5. How has following this path changed your life?

After the pandemic, my husband and I began joining Shabbat dinners and services at Chabad. What started occasionally soon became part of our lives. Chabad became a center for us, a place of learning and friendship. Especially after October 7, 2023, more people began showing up, and a new circle of friends grew out of that difficult time.

This path has changed the way I see the world. I think less about myself and more about others. I try to meet people with compassion, knowing that every interaction matters to G-d. Relationships are sacred.

I feel more gratitude now, not only for big blessings but also for the small, everyday moments. Even challenges feel like opportunities to grow. I am learning to let go of control and trust that G-d runs the world. That trust brings peace.

Daily life feels different. I try to bring the Divine into the ordinary. I follow the Jewish calendar and prepare for the holidays, knowing they carry deep meaning. As a Noahide I respect the limits of observance, but within those boundaries I have found depth and purpose.

6. What are you currently learning?

My studies continue to expand. Each week I attend Torah classes with our Rabbi. I study Hebrew and meet regularly with two observant Jewish women, as well as with my Noahide *chavrusa.*[52]

I've studied *Shaar HaBitachon (The Gate of Faith),* and *The Divine Code* and *Seven Gates of Righteous Knowledge* by Rabbi Moshe Weiner. Right now, I'm reading *The Garden of Emuna.*

Daily, I read *Psalms* and *The Daily Companion on Lashon Hara*[53] by the Chafetz Chaim. The focus on guarding speech is especially important. I also listen to Torah lectures from many different Rabbis. The learning never stops, thank G-d.

7. How do you apply what you learn to your daily life?

I have a prayer practice and recite blessings throughout the day, before eating, drinking, and even after using the bathroom. Modesty has been part of my life for some time, but now I approach it with greater awareness and intention. Each morning I wake up and thank Hashem for the gift of a new day and for the opportunity to be of service and to do good in a world that is so often troubled.

---

52. The word in Hebrew for "study partner".

53. *Lashon hara* is the term in Hebrew for "sinful speech" which one says about another person (for example, gossip).

This journey has made me more giving and more attentive to the needs of others. I try to choose my words carefully, strengthen my relationships, and work on my character traits. I want to be clear that this path is a practice. It does not mean I do things perfectly or that I have somehow erased all my flaws. What it means is that I am more aware of my actions, words, and thoughts. I am learning, especially in difficult or uncomfortable situations, to pause and interrupt old patterns.

Most of all, I see life itself as an opportunity to elevate. Every moment and every choice is a chance to bring holiness into the world. We are here to bring Heaven down to earth, refining ourselves and our relationships along the way. While the Jewish people are here to bring the light of Torah into the world, our path as Noahides is to be inspired by that light and to share it with others. We may not carry the same covenant, but we are given the privilege of reflecting its wisdom in our own lives. By living with integrity, kindness, and awareness of Hashem, we help make that light visible beyond the Jewish community. In this way, we can support and honor the mission of Israel while also contributing to the sanctification of the world in our own measure.

This path has given me a map for living, one that helps me make each day count.

KEY LESSONS

1. **The search for truth is never wasted.** Every spiritual path I explored, from Buddhism to alchemical fire circles, shaped my understanding and prepared me to recognize the depth of Torah when I finally encountered it.

2. **One moment can change everything.** Hearing *Bereishit* read aloud for the first time awakened something in me. Sometimes, a single experience is enough to redirect the course of a life.

3. **Learning Torah brings clarity and connection.** During the chaos of the world, Torah became my ark. It gave me purpose, stability, and a deeper bond with my husband as we explored its wisdom together.

4. **Community is a gift, not a given.** Many Noahides struggle to find a supportive environment, but I have been blessed with a strong welcoming Chabad community. Being part of it has deepened my learning and my connection with G-d.

5. **Spirituality is about integration, not separation.** Spirituality isn't something separate from daily life. I live by the Jewish calendar, incorporating its rhythms into my home, my meals, and my mindset.

6. **The more you learn, the more you grow.** My journey has led me to constant study of Hebrew, Torah, and Jewish ethics, and with each new lesson, my connection to this path deepens.

7. **Life is meant to be elevated, through Torah.** I've learned that every moment holds meaning. Every action, every choice is an opportunity to bring holiness into the world and live with greater purpose.

21.

Katy Holladay | (USA)

HOW TORAH TRANSFORMED MY LIFE

"Hashem doesn't demand blind faith;
He invites us to seek, question, and discover Him
through wisdom and understanding."

1. What is your background?

My background is pretty interesting. My parents were Christians, but my dad didn't become a Christian until he was in his late teens or early twenties. It was a very personal experience for him, one of those "I had an encounter" moments. Since he didn't grow up in a traditional Christian setting, he was always a truth seeker, constantly asking questions. After he became involved in church, met my mother, and got married, they spent a lot of time in Bible study, with a particular focus on the Torah. My father would often ask, "Why don't we do this, if this is what the Bible says?" The answers he received from pastors and church leaders were never fully satisfying. As a result, our family always approached faith a little differently.

When we moved to another town due to my dad's job, it provided a natural break. We started asking more questions, wondering if we had been told the truth about Christianity. We tried different churches, searching for something that made sense, but nothing fit. It was like Hashem was pulling us in a different direction. Looking back, I see it as Divine orchestration; Hashem was gradually leading us out.

A turning point came when my dad started working at a local Christian television station. The owner of the station was deeply interested in Israel and became involved with the Temple Institute. This put him in contact with Rabbi Chaim Richman, whom he invited to Texas to speak about the Temple and its significance.

Eventually, when I was old enough, I started working at the station as well, along with several of my siblings. Because of this, I had direct access to the teachings of Rabbi Richman and others who shared perspectives on Torah that I had never encountered before. I worked behind the scenes, running cameras and assisting with production, which meant that I had no choice but to listen to the teachings being shared. I always say Hashem orchestrates our lives, and in this case, He quite literally placed me in a position where I had to sit through Torah classes!

If you've ever met Rabbi Richman, you know how captivating he is, such an inspiring teacher. During my time at the station, I had the chance to get to know him, as well as another Jewish teacher named Sam Peak, of blessed memory, who fondly called himself "the Jewish Cowboy." Sam led classes, and it was through him that I was first introduced to Torah study, beginning with the book *Derech Hashem*[54].

2. How did you discover the Seven Laws of Noah?

The transition happened gradually. Because of his job at the Christian television station, my dad was exposed to discussions that challenged traditional Christian beliefs. The station aired

---

54. *Derech Hashem (The Way of G-d)* is a classic work of Jewish philosophy and ethics by Rabbi Moshe Chaim Luzzatto (Ramchal), written in the 18th century. It presents a systematic overview of fundamental Torah principles, including the purpose of creation, Divine providence, prophecy, and the structure of the spiritual world.

national pastors but also had its own programming, including discussions about Israel and the Temple.

That exposure was incredibly important for my development on this path. At first, my journey took me through Messianic Judaism, which seemed like a natural step for someone coming out of Christianity but still holding onto certain beliefs. However, the more I studied, the more I realized that I was still trying to fit into a framework that didn't align with what I was learning. I felt torn, on one hand, I was still attached to the ideas I had grown up with, but on the other, the Torah's truth was undeniable.

With the support and guidance of Rabbi Richman and Sam Peak, I was able to step away from Messianic beliefs completely. I put Jesus on the shelf and started focusing on my own path. One of the most powerful things Rabbi Richman ever said to me was, "The Torah is for everyone, and everyone is in the Torah, so go and find yourself." That moment changed everything for me.

That's when I discovered the Seven Noahide Laws. I came across teachings that explained how these Laws provide a moral and spiritual foundation for all of humanity. I realized that I didn't need to convert to Judaism to have a meaningful relationship with Hashem, because I already had a role to fulfill as a Noahide. Since then, my journey has been about deepening that understanding. The Seven Laws are about living with purpose, recognizing Hashem in everything, and striving to be a better person every day.

Now, my parents are also Noahides, and three of my sisters are, too. I have two brothers who got married and returned to Christianity for the sake of their wives. I'm married as well and have two children. My husband does not label himself as a Noahide, but he's an honorable man who essentially lives by Noahide principles. However, he's not interested in spirituality, and that's just not for him. We have an understanding that his spiritual walk is his and mine is mine, and we don't interfere with each other's beliefs. Everyone should have their own personal relationship with Hashem.

3. What impact did this knowledge have on you?

Learning about the Seven Laws of Noah gave me a framework for understanding my faith and life in a way that Christianity never did. It has shaped how I see people, how I treat others, and how I conduct myself in business and relationships. I learned to appreciate the significance of kindness, honesty, and integrity in everyday life. It's also given me a deeper appreciation for Hashem's role in the world.

Understanding Hashem's presence has allowed me to feel more connected, not just to Him, but to the world and the people around me. It has helped me navigate difficult situations with more compassion and patience. I've realized that every interaction is an opportunity to bring light into the world. Even something as small as treating someone with kindness, giving someone the benefit of the doubt, or being honest in a difficult situation can create a ripple effect.

Another major impact has been my perspective on the value of everyday life. In Christianity, the focus was often on the afterlife, what happens when we die, where we go, and whether we are "saved." But the Noahide path emphasizes the sanctity of this life, of what we do in the here and now. I no longer feel like I'm just waiting for some distant reward. I see the purpose in the small, mundane moments.

4. What has been your biggest challenge?

The biggest challenge is getting over the fear of letting go of former beliefs, especially when you've been raised in Christianity since childhood. There's an underlying fear: "If I stop believing, will I go to hell?" You have to unlearn some things and replace them with truth. That process is not just intellectual, it's emotional. You're dismantling an entire framework that shaped your identity, your relationships, and the way you understood the world.

It took time to recognize that my fear wasn't coming from Hashem but from years of conditioning. I had to ask myself: "Why would a just and merciful G-d punish someone for seeking truth?" The more I studied, the more I saw that those fears were unfounded. But letting go was still difficult. There's a sense of grief when you realize that what you believed for so long isn't true. At the same time, there's an incredible sense of relief when you finally align with what is true.

You also have to deal with the reactions of family and friends. Some people lose relationships over it. I've seen so many Noahides burn bridges by being too abrupt, cutting people off, or attacking Christianity instead of simply explaining their personal journey. That approach only creates more division. It's important to be gentle and understand that change is hard for everyone.

I watched my father navigate this as well. He learned early on that the best way to handle it was to lead by example, not by argument. He never forced his beliefs on my mother, respecting her spiritual process while remaining steadfast in his own. That lesson has stayed with me, and I now see that love and respect are more important than demanding that others see the world as I do.

Another challenge has been shifting how I think. My teacher, Sam Peak, used to say, "You have to change the way you think." That stuck with me. Christianity taught me to see things in a very specific way, putting faith over reason, submission over questioning. But Judaism and the Noahide path encourage questions. They value understanding over blind belief. I had to rewire my mindset to embrace critical thinking, trust that Hashem wants us to seek truth, and realize that faith isn't about suppressing doubt but about engaging with it.

Finally, there's the challenge of isolation. I don't live in a large Jewish or Noahide community, so much of my learning has been independent. While I have online mentors and study groups, there's still something missing when you don't have a physical community to share experiences with. I've had to find ways to stay connected, whether through Zoom classes, discussions with my family, or engaging with others on social media.

5. How has following this path changed your life?

This journey has deepened my understanding of what it means to trust Hashem's plan, not just for myself but for others. I used to feel the need to convince people of what I had learned, but I've come to see that everyone's relationship with Hashem is their own. I have learned that Hashem tailors each life individually, orchestrating experiences in ways we might not immediately recognize.

Through this, I have also developed a new appreciation for relationships. I understand the importance of maintaining peace in my home and not putting my own ego between my spouse and me, using Hashem as an excuse.

Another major shift has been in how I perceive struggles. I no longer see challenges as obstacles but as opportunities to grow, to refine myself, and to develop resilience. I've come to understand that the mundane, seemingly insignificant moments of life are where Hashem is most present. Whether it's doing laundry, running errands, or simply being there for my children, these are the moments where I can serve Him.

On difficult days, when I feel overwhelmed or unable to battle my inner struggles, I remind myself of what the Torah says: "For there is a hand on the throne of Hashem: Hashem maintains a war against Amalek from generation to generation."[55] Even when I feel weak, Hashem fights on my behalf. Knowing this has allowed me to let go of guilt, trust in Divine timing, and keep moving forward with faith.

6. What are you currently learning?

Right now, I'm studying personal refinement and character development. I focus on Torah teachings that emphasize inner work, how to refine myself, how to be more aware of Hashem's presence in my life, and how to grow spiritually. I'm taking continuing education courses in energy therapy with Rebbetzin Orit Ester Riter of the Or Emuna institute and also follow my rabbi's weekly Torah teachings.

I've found that the more I study, the more I realize how much there is to learn. I've learned to be alright with things I don't fully understand yet, knowing that Hashem reveals knowledge at the right time. A lot of my studies revolve around self-improvement, not just in a broad sense, but in a very real, practical way.

One of the most transformative ideas I've learned is that our spiritual journey is not just about what we know, but about how we change. Rabbi Yitzchak Ginsburgh's book *Wisdom for the Nations* helped me see the deeper dimensions of the Noahide Laws. Instead of viewing them as a set of external rules, I now understand that they have an inner dimension that calls us to transform ourselves. For example, the commandment to avoid idolatry isn't just about not worshiping false gods; it's about working on yourself diligently, continually involving yourself on self-improvement and self-refinement.

---

55. Exodus 17:16.

7. How do you apply what you learn to your daily life?

Every interaction is an opportunity to apply Torah wisdom. In my work as an energy therapist, most of my clients are Jewish, so I sit in this unique space where I understand both the Jewish and non-Jewish perspectives. I see how intention transforms actions.

I also teach my children about Hashem, though I let them develop their own relationship with Him. I tell them, "Hashem is not Santa Claus; He's here to support and guide you, not just to make everything easy."

One of the most meaningful concepts I've internalized is the idea that even our struggles and mundane tasks matter. When Jacob wrestled with Esau's angel, the sages say the dust from their struggle rose up to Heaven as a pleasing aroma to Hashem. That taught me that even the small, seemingly insignificant battles in life have meaning.

Overall, I strive to be a source of light wherever I go, knowing that even the smallest efforts can create ripples of goodness in the world.

KEY LESSONS

1. **Truth is a journey, not a destination.** My father's search for truth shaped my own. I wasn't looking for a new path, just answers. But those answers led me out of Christianity and into Torah study, where I discovered the Seven Noahide Laws. Seeking truth is an ongoing journey that requires courage, patience, and humility.

2. **Hashem orchestrates every step.** Looking back, I see how, through my dad's job, my exposure to Torah, Rabbi Richman and Sam Peak was no coincidence. Every step, even working behind the camera at a TV station, was part of Hashem's plan, leading me to where I needed to be.

3. **Letting go of the past is both terrifying and liberating.** Overcoming the fear of leaving Christianity was one of my biggest struggles. The idea of going to hell had been ingrained in me. But when I stopped looking for someone else to define my faith, I felt an incredible sense of peace.

4. **Not everyone will understand, and that's alright.** Some family members returned to Christianity, while I continued on my path. I saw others burn bridges by being too confrontational, and I knew I wanted to handle it differently. My father's example taught me to respect others' journeys, just as I want mine to be respected.

5. **Small actions carry deep spiritual meaning.** Christianity emphasized the afterlife, but Torah taught me that Hashem is within everyday life. Kindness, honesty, and integrity matter in every interaction. Even mundane struggles and daily routines hold deep spiritual significance.

6. **Faith and reason must work together.** Christianity told me to believe without questioning, but Torah taught me to engage critically. Sam Peak used to say, "You have to change the way you think." Real faith isn't blind; it's built through learning, reasoning, and seeking truth.

7. **I don't have to convert the world, only improve myself.** At first, I wanted to share my discoveries with everyone, but I realized my role isn't to convince others. My job is to live with honesty and kindness, trusting that my actions, not debates, will make an impact.

22.

Jim Long | (USA)

FROM FAITHFUL SEARCHER TO NOAHIDE ADVOCATE

*"Everything that happens to us comes from G-d,
but our free will lies in how we respond to it.
By living righteously, we align ourselves with His will,
and bring peace to our own hearts."*

1. What is your background?

I was born in rural Missouri but spent my childhood moving around the United States. Some of my most vivid memories are from Northern and Southern California, Oregon, Indiana, and Texas. We frequently relocated because my father was an "exhibitor" a title given to movie theater managers back in the 1950s. This meant I practically grew up in darkened theaters, letting my imagination run wild.

Thanks to my mother, of blessed memory, I also had a strong belief in G-d. She was Protestant, though not particularly devout, but she believed in G-d and wanted her children to have a strong moral foundation. She enrolled my brother and me in Catholic school, hoping it would provide us with discipline and a connection to faith, even though she wasn't Catholic herself.

Years later, I asked her, "Why did you enroll us in a parochial school even though you weren't Catholic?" She told me, "We have a saying in America about the three R's: reading, writing, and 'rithmetic. But I wanted you boys to have four R's: reading, writing, 'rithmetic, and religion." She didn't feel capable of teaching us about G-d, but she wanted us to know He existed.

While I was still in kindergarten, we moved from California to Indiana but the Catholic school there lacked a preschool of any kind so I was placed with first graders. Even then I was the kid with his nose in a book. Curiosity has been a lifelong habit that included film, especially since the movies were my second home. If I saw a film that intrigued me, I would read everything I could about the story behind it, whether it was about Rome, volcanoes, or ancient civilizations. This curiosity gave me a voracious love for reading and learning. No surprise, that I was drawn to the bookcase in our living room, filled with my mother's favorite mystery novels. The book that aroused my curiosity the most was the Bible. Soon, I immersed myself in what I once knew as the Old Testament.

As a Catholic, I was not encouraged to read the Bible, only the catechism. By the time I was a teenager, I had begun questioning Catholicism, especially after I learned about the Spanish Inquisition. I thought, "That's not a Church of G-d. It cannot be." That realization led me to leave Catholicism and explore other religions. I sought the truth in Protestant denominations, looking for clarity and answers I couldn't find in the traditions I grew up with. This spiritual curiosity stayed with me, driving me to study the Bible, history, and archaeology with an insatiable hunger for understanding.

2. How did you discover the Seven Laws of Noah?

It was a winding, often painful journey that began when I was about eight or nine years old. I have a vivid memory of a lovely summer day, stretched out on the cool grass staring up at the sky, thinking about G-d. I didn't know why, but I felt completely overwhelmed by the thought that G-d was bigger than the sky. That realization scared the dickens out of me. In retrospect, it felt like my "Abraham moment."

During high school, I dated a girl whose parents would only allow me to see her if I attended their congregation. They were Church of Christ, a denomination that typically ignored the so-called Old Testament, which had always been my favorite part of the Bible. When they brought in a minister who taught it with real passion, it rekindled my interest in what I now know as the *Torah, Prophets* and *Writings.* However, the leaders of the congregation believed the minister was misguided and fired him. I took it as a sign that they were the ones who were misguided.

In my early thirties, I worked at a radio station in Waco, Texas, where I managed programming. During this time, I became deeply involved in a Christian cult called Holy Ground Mission. At first, it seemed like a place where I, my wife and two children, could find community and spiritual depth. Tom, the leader of the cult, was a charismatic former magician who claimed to have unique insight into the Bible. Paradoxically, his teachings were my introduction to Torah and Shabbat observance, yet he harbored deeply antisemitic views. He twisted Biblical texts to subtly vilify Jewish people. I now realize that this man was willfully ignorant of basic Torah concepts. Tom believed that converts were not truly Jews and characterized them as evil interlopers! He didn't understand that Avraham was promised that his descendants would become a great nation (*Genesis 12:2*) and that the Torah embraces the convert who joins the nation. According to Torah, converts are halachically a citizen in a very literal sense. (*Leviticus 19:34*), while some Jewish mystical teachings suggest that a convert has returned to their destiny.

After four years, we left the cult. Our departure from Holy Ground Mission marked the beginning of a new path that eventually led me to Vendyl Jones, a Texas-based archaeologist and Bible scholar known for his efforts to find the Ark of the Covenant. I met him during my time at a Dallas broadcast station with a talk-radio format. He was a last-minute replacement for a guest who had canceled unexpectedly. During the interview, it was clear that he possessed a passion for Torah, archaeology, and uncovering Biblical mysteries. Following the interview, Vendyl invited me to his Torah classes, and from the very first session, I was hooked, delving deeper and finding that every fundamental of Torah hit me at my core.

Vendyl was unlike anyone I had met. His knowledge of the Bible was deep and profound, but what truly struck me was his respect for the Jewish tradition. Through his teachings, I was introduced fully into the Torah, as well as the Seven Laws of Noah, a universal framework for living a righteous life. For the first time, I felt like I had found clarity and a connection to the Creator that transcended religious boundaries.

3. What impact did this knowledge have on you?

Learning about the Seven Laws of Noah reshaped my understanding of the nature of G-d and what He expects from humanity. I realized that these universal principles were not just rules but a Divine blueprint for justice, morality, and peace. This knowledge also helped me shed the harmful teachings of the cult. I began to see the Jewish people as the carriers of Divine wisdom. Every time I studied Torah, I felt like I was uncovering truths that had been buried inside me all along. Occasionally, I would have what felt like small revelations, and I'd verify them with learned scholars. This transformation extended to my relationships as well. My youngest son, Paul, has turned to me with questions about Torah. Those conversations have deepened the bond between us. My older son, Jordan, discovered much-needed understanding after our time in the cult. I showed him the simplicity of G-d's requirements for humanity: "Follow the Seven Laws and practice charity. In doing so, you're squared away with the Creator." That straightforward truth gave him a foundation to rebuild his faith.

4. What has been your biggest challenge?

There were several challenges. The first was accepting the Oral Torah. Coming from a Christian background that emphasized "sola scriptura" (scripture alone), I struggled with the idea of relying on traditions not explicitly written in the Bible. It felt foreign and even untrustworthy at first. Through study, I began to understand that the Oral Torah is essential for the observant Jew who strives to apply the meaning of the text. For example, the commandment to observe Shabbat is found in the Written Torah, but it's the Oral Torah that explains how to keep it. The same holds true for other commandments, such as *tefillin* (phylacteries), kashering the meat of an animal, maintaining family ritual purity, the mezuzah, etc. Accepting this was a pivotal in my spiritual growth.

The second challenge was coming to terms with the idea that I don't need to convert to live a righteous life before G-d. For a long time, I wanted to convert, believing that was the only way to fully embrace Torah. But I learned that living according to the Noachide Laws was exactly what G-d wanted from me.

The third hurdle was finding a partner who understood and respected this path. Before I met my wife Carol, I invited the women I dated to Torah classes so as to gauge their reactions. Most of them were confused or dismissive. But when I took Carol to a class, she simply said, "That was really interesting." She was a Christian but had left the church because she had too many unanswered questions. Through Torah study, she found those answers, and we had a Noahide wedding.

5. How has following this path changed your life?

There was a crucial turning point that came a few years before I met Carol, even prior to getting acquainted with Vendyl. It was when I decided to change my name. Shortly after leaving the cult my world fell apart. I lost my job and I went through a divorce. My life was in ruins. That is when I thought of the story in the Torah where G-d changes the names of Sarah and Avraham, and in doing so changes their destinies. When I was fifteen, I was shown my original birth certificate and learned that the man who had raised me was actually my stepfather. Thankfully, he was a very good father to me, and I am deeply grateful for that.

Faced with an uncertain future, I decided to reclaim my birth name. Within a short time, the decision felt like a realignment with who I truly was. My life took a decisive turn. I moved to Dallas, Texas, and stepped into a career in talk radio. Looking back, I am convinced that embracing my true identity eventually brought me to Torah. G-d had used Vendyl in that respect. I am just as certain that my journey could only continue with Carol by my side.

One day in 1994, I was walking the streets of Jerusalem and marveled that I was trodding the same land as the Biblical patriarchs and even participating in an archaeological dig. I was experiencing a life that I never could have imagined a few years earlier. It may sound melodramatic but I believe that I had found my true destiny. In Carol, I had met my Sarah.

Torah taught me to be a better husband. I learned that women are on a higher spiritual plane than men. G-d told Abraham, "Whatever Sarah tells you, heed her voice." In Christianity, women are often seen as subordinate, but Torah elevates them. That understanding transformed my marriage and my perspective on relationships.

6. What are you currently learning?

I'm currently focused on the weekly Torah parsha and writing a blog for Jerusalem Lights, where I explore historical and spiritual insights. I also co-host the Jerusalem Lights podcast with my dear friend Rabbi Chaim Richman, where we take deep dives into these topics from both Jewish and Noahide perspectives.

I've authored two books, *Riddle of the Exodus,* and the latest, *Blood Brother: Israel's Ancient Enemy.* The former resulted in a series of lectures to mostly Orthodox Jewish audiences across the U.S., including New York, Chicago, Boston, Baltimore, San Diego and San Antonio. In addition, I have spoken in London and in Jerusalem. These venues have been an opportunity to share my experiences as a Ben Noah. I always tell my audience that if the whole world embraced the Seven Noahide Laws, peace would break out overnight. That's all G-d wants.

I am primarily a filmmaker, having written and produced two documentaries, "Riddle of the Exodus" as well as "Treasures of the Copper Scroll." They reflect my lifelong pursuit of Biblical truth. I also get my hands dirty in archaeological digs in Israel, which keeps me connected to Israel's history.

Through Torah study, archaeology, and Biblical research, my goal is to bridge the past with the present, to bring history to life and help others see the incredible depth and relevance of the Torah in today's world.

7. How do you apply what you learn to your daily life?

The most profound lesson I've learned is that everything in life comes from G-d, but our free will lies in how we respond to it. This understanding has shaped how I approach challenges, setbacks, and even tragedies.

Each day, I strive to live by the Seven Laws of Noah, focusing on acts of charity, kindness, and justice. Supporting Israel, sharing knowledge, and helping others are central to my mission. *B'esrat HaShem* (With G-d's help) I continue to follow what I believe is the path that He has set before me.

Studying Torah has become a continuous process of discovery and self-improvement. It's not just about gaining knowledge, it's about applying that wisdom to life. Whether I'm writing, teaching, or engaging in meaningful conversations, I aim to live righteously and help others do the same.

Looking back, I can see how every step of my journey, both the highs and the lows, was part of G-d's plan. I often remind myself that the Creator's purpose is far greater than we can comprehend. By embracing the challenges and blessings He sends, I've found clarity, purpose, and peace. To anyone searching for meaning, I would say: *Trust the process. G-d's hand is in everything, and by choosing righteousness, we align ourselves with His will.*

KEY LESSONS

1. **G-d's plan is bigger than I can understand.** Life's twists and turns, even the most painful ones, are all part of a Divine plan. Looking back, I can see how every challenge was necessary to bring me to where I am today. Trusting that everything happens for a reason has helped me find clarity and peace.

2. **My free will lies in how I respond.** While everything that happens comes from G-d, how I respond defines who I am. Choosing kindness, charity, and justice in the face of life's challenges brings me closer to my true purpose and strengthens my connection to the Creator.

3. **Embracing universal principles has brought me clarity.** The Seven Laws of Noah are a guide to living a meaningful and righteous life. Studying Torah has given me a sense of direction and a deeper understanding of what it means to walk in righteousness.

4. **It's never too late to transform.** Whether it's through changing my name, shifting careers, or embracing a new spiritual path, I've learned that transformation is possible at any stage of life. Realigning with my true purpose has led to unexpected opportunities and personal growth.

5. **Knowledge is meant to be shared.** Teaching, writing, and engaging with others is a responsibility I take seriously. By sharing what I've learned, I hope to help others find clarity and purpose in their own journeys, creating a ripple effect of righteousness in the world.

6. **Growth comes from questioning and seeking.** My spiritual journey has been shaped by curiosity and a willingness to question my upbringing. The search for truth has led me to a deeper wisdom that I never could have imagined when I first started my journey.

7. **True faith requires action.** Faith demands action. I strive to live by moral principles, practice kindness, and make ethical choices every day because these actions bring faith to life and create a lasting impact on those around me.

23.

Sebastian ben Noah | (Germany)

HIDDEN IN PLAIN SIGHT

"I live a quiet life with a very loud truth."

1. What is your background?

I was raised in a small town near Munich, Germany. My upbringing was rooted in strong values, though not tied to any religion. My parents taught me right from wrong; things like don't steal, be kind and work hard, which, in hindsight, aligned well with the Noahide Laws. As a teen, I briefly got involved in church youth work but left when I started questioning its relevance. The pastor spoke disparagingly about rock music, including several bands I liked. That judgment turned me off. I was much more drawn to philosophy than to church doctrine. When I read Nietzsche's *Thus Spoke Zarathustra*, I knew I was looking for something deeper. I just didn't know yet what it was.

2. How did you discover the Seven Laws of Noah?

In 1999, I was practicing martial arts with a teacher in Munich who had been inspired by the Lubavitcher Rebbe to spread the Noahide Code. He offered a free seminar to his students. That's where I heard about the Seven Laws for the first time. It wasn't just the content that struck me, it was the authenticity. No one was trying to "sell" me anything. I felt like I had found something honest, ancient, and true. He recommended I read *Shaar HaYichud*

VehaEmuna (The Gate of Unity and Faith), which is the second section of *Tanya*[56]. That's when my real journey began.

3. What impact did this knowledge have on you?

It became my foundation for everything. I changed what I watched, gave more to charity, and stayed away from churches. I started to think differently, live more ethically, and apply the Laws to every part of my life. The moral clarity helped me make better choices, especially about what I expose myself to, whether that be media or people. I'm more careful about what I say, more aware of my actions, and more grounded overall. I know where my moral compass is. I keep much of it private, though, I don't really talk about being a Noahide, because in today's culture, especially in Germany, openly supporting Israel or talking about G-d and Judaism can get you socially "canceled." I don't want that.

4. What has been your biggest challenge?

The loneliness. I'm still not married. I'm looking for someone who's in alignment with this path, but that's incredibly rare. Staying true to this path has meant saying no to relationships that didn't honor it. That's hard. But compromising would be worse. Also, not being able to study certain Torah topics as a Noahide, it's sad. There's so much beauty, and I want to delve into it. Thank G-d for teachers like Dr. Michael Schulman from Asknoah.org, who guide me through what's appropriate.

---

56. This second section of *Tanya* is especially recommended for Noahides.

5. How has following this path changed your life?

It's saved me from a lot of trouble. I don't use drugs, I don't waste my life on shallow relationships, and I don't fall into spiritual traps. In the past, I may have been tempted by things that would cause me to sin, but the Noahide Laws have given me a spiritual spine. Even to avoid something as "simple" as *lashon hara*[57], I'm constantly working on guarding my speech. Without these teachings, I'd likely be wandering, spiritually and emotionally. I feel that I live with clarity, discipline, and dignity. It's not always easy, but it's deeply fulfilling.

6. What are you currently learning?

Right now I'm learning from *The Divine Code*, *Tanya*, *Chofetz Chaim: A Lesson a Day*, and Torah with commentaries. I also enjoy books recommended by Dr. Schulman, like *Kindness* by Rabbi Zelig Pliskin. I have a real love for language, Hebrew especially, and I'm currently reading the Soncino *Chumash* in both Hebrew and English. I also picked up a book called *A Moment of Silence* by Abraham Frank, which explores the power of reflection in public schools. My bookshelf is sacred space. I surround myself with these books because they keep me anchored.

7. How do you apply what you learn to your daily life?

I start each day with prayer. I actively work on not speaking negatively. I try to think well of people, avoid resentment, and be mindful of my words. I don't consume unethical media or support

---

57. *Lashon hara* is the term in Hebrew for "sinful speech" which one says about another person (for example, gossip).

ideas that go against this path. I give *tzedakah*[58]. I try to uplift others, even subtly, like asking a colleague, "Why is your face so downcast today?" as Josef[59] did in prison. Most people aren't open to religion, so I translate spiritual wisdom into everyday language. Let your actions speak. That's what I try to live by.

58. *Tzedakah* is the Hebrew word for charity. It comes from the root *tzedek*, meaning "justice" or "righteousness." In Judaism, giving to those in need is seen as fulfilling a moral obligation to act justly.

59. See Genesis 40:7.

KEY LESSONS

1. **You don't need a label to live with truth.** I didn't grow up religious, but once I encountered the Seven Laws, everything clicked. Sometimes truth just feels like home.

2. **Authenticity doesn't need a sales pitch.** The Noahide path wasn't "marketed" to me. That's how I knew it was real. When something is genuine, it speaks for itself.

3. **Isolation is painful, but integrity is non-negotiable.** I'm still searching for a life partner. It's lonely, but I refuse to dishonor what I know is right just to fill the loneliness.

4. **What you don't say matters just as much as what you do.** *Lashon hara* has been one of the hardest battles, and the most important. I'm learning to guard my tongue like it's sacred.

5. **Silence can be sacred, for now.** I conceal my Noahide identity for safety, not shame. In this cultural moment, silence protects me so I can live as a Noahide, develop my thoughts, and subtly spread Torah light. For now, it is good to conceal.

6. **You can live the truth without shouting it.** I've learned to embed Torah values into ordinary speech. "Why is your face downcast today?" is a holy question, even in German.

7. **The deed is everything.** *Ha'maaseh hu ha'ikar* ("the action is the main thing"). You don't need to preach. Just do good. That's the best kind of teaching.

24.

Pamela bat Noah | (USA)

EVEN IN THE FIRE, I CLING TO HIM

"Even in the hardest parts of my life, abuse, addiction, poverty, and grief, I never stopped believing in G-d. I just didn't yet know who He really was."

1. What is your background?

I didn't grow up with safety. I grew up with survival. My mom was there, but emotionally checked out. When I found the courage to speak up about being molested by her boyfriend, her response wasn't to protect me; it was to send me and my brothers to live with our grandmother. That's when the cycle of displacement started. We bounced through foster care and group homes. By the time I was a teenager, I was mostly raising myself and my siblings. I also knew how to keep my guard up, and how to pretend like I was fine when I wasn't.

But even in all that darkness, I felt G-d. I couldn't explain it. As a child, I would sit on my bed and read the Bible like a regular book, cover to cover. I started at the beginning, and I noticed things. Things that didn't add up. People said JC was G-d, but the words didn't support that. Even as a kid, I could feel something was off. I didn't know what I was looking for, but I knew what I was reading didn't match what I was being taught.

As I got older, the hardship only deepened. I ended up in abusive relationships. I had children young, without a real sense of what it meant to be mothered myself. I struggled with addiction and landed in jail. I went through treatment and worked hard to rebuild, but I had no family to fall back on. I got by through grit and the constant belief that there had to be more than this. That G-d had a plan for me.

2. How did you discover the Seven Laws of Noah?

It happened when I was in a relationship with a Jewish man. I was still very Christian at the time, very much on that mission mindset, but I was also curious. I respected Judaism. I knew the Jewish people were called "chosen," and I wanted to understand why they didn't accept JC. So, my boyfriend and I, we started studying together. At some point, we watched a video debate between a rabbi and a Christian pastor. Not even halfway through, I knew, deep in my soul, that what I had believed was false. I felt betrayed, lied to. I even had tattoos of crosses that would itch and bleed. Once I had them covered up, the itching stopped. That wasn't just physical. That was spiritual.

From there, I stepped fully into the Jewish world. I lived as an Orthodox woman. I kept Torah law, covered my hair, kept kosher, and observed Shabbat. I was ready to convert and become Jewish.

But then a rabbi told me something I did not expect: "You don't have to convert to serve G-d." That was the first time I heard about the Seven Laws of Noah. At first, I struggled with it. Was this a compromise? Was it somehow less? But the more I learned, the more I understood that it was not a lesser path at all. It was *my* path.

3. What impact did this knowledge have on you?

It gave me peace. It gave me a way to serve Hashem with integrity, without pretending to be someone I'm not. I still live with modesty. I still honor the seventh day with candles, a meal, and quiet. Not because I have to, but because I want to. These are my offerings of respect. My way of saying, "You, Hashem, are the center of my life."

It also gave me clarity. I could finally understand what I had sensed as a child, that the confusion I felt in Christianity wasn't my fault. It was real. And I wasn't crazy or rebellious for walking away.

4. What has been your biggest challenge?

Loneliness. Isolation. Feeling like I don't belong anywhere. There's no Noahide community where I live. No one I can talk to who understands this path. Most people don't even know what a Noahide is. My kids go to public school, and I've had to teach them to stand up for what we believe in, even when other kids don't understand.

But the deepest challenge has been carrying everything alone. My husband died suddenly. Just didn't show up to work. Gone. And now, the man I'm with, the one I believe is truly my soulmate, is in prison. I can't visit him. I get fifteen-minute calls a couple times a week. And I'm here, raising three kids, running a business, trying not to fall apart. Some days I feel like I'm barely hanging on. But I remind myself: Hashem gave me this life. He must know I can handle it.

5. How has following this path changed your life?

It gave me my life back. I used to be addicted to all kinds of things, alcohol, chaos, pain. Even religion itself, at one point. But the Noahide path gave me balance. It gave me boundaries and structure without the crushing weight of a system that wasn't made for me. It gave me a direct relationship with G-d.

I now look at everything that happens, good or bad, and ask, "What's the message here?" If something breaks, I thank Hashem for giving someone else a job to fix it. If plans fall through, I believe it's Divine protection. That shift in thinking changes everything.

And I've passed it on to my kids. They know we don't celebrate certain holidays, and they know why. They know how to say "no" respectfully. I remind them: we are leaders, not followers. And we honor Hashem not just with words, but with how we live.

6. What are you currently learning?

Right now, I'm learning how to keep going. After my husband died, I fell back into some old habits. I started smoking again. I haven't been studying like I used to. But I'm trying. I'm learning that the *yetzer hara*[60] doesn't always tempt you with sin. Sometimes, it just wants to make you feel worthless. Make you give up. That's the battle I'm in. I'm learning to fight back with gratitude. To say thank You for the mess. To thank Hashem for the chaos, because it means I'm still here.

7. How do you apply what you learn to your daily life?

I run a business serving mostly Jewish clients. I walk around in a headscarf and modest clothing in a place where almost no one does that. I light candles every Friday night. I teach my kids to be proud of our path, even when it means being different.

And I give where I can. I donate to Noahide projects because I want to help others find this path, especially people in prison. Right now, they are usually offered Christianity or Islam, but I believe there should also be a third option, a universal path.

I dream of starting a Noahide resource center where I live. Maybe a food pantry, a school supplies program, a small gathering group, something that can truly help people.I want to build something that lasts.

---

60. The term in Hebrew for a person's "bad inclination".

KEY LESSONS

1. **G-d was with me even before I knew who He was.** I was reading the Bible as a kid and asking questions that no one around me could answer. I didn't have the vocabulary yet, but I knew something was off. That was Hashem planting seeds in my soul before I even knew who He was.

2. **The truth can hurt, but it also heals.** When I realized everything I believed growing up was false, it broke me. But it also freed me. I stopped clinging to what didn't make sense. Truth is painful sometimes, but it's the only thing worth living for.

3. **I don't need to be Jewish to serve Hashem with my whole heart.** I lived as a Hasidic woman for years. I was serious about converting. But learning about the Noahide path helped me see that I could honor G-d without becoming a Jew. I serve Him as I am, and it's real.

4. **Honoring the seventh day and dressing modestly are my offerings of respect.** I know I'm not commanded to do these things, but I choose to light candles, sit with my kids, and keep the seventh day special. I cover my hair and dress modestly not out of obligation, but out of awe. This is how I show reverence to the One I serve.

5. ***Emuna* means showing up when you have nothing left.** Some days I feel like I'm barely holding on. I've buried a husband, and I'm in a long-distance relationship with my fiancé who's in prison. I run a business and raise my kids alone. But I still say "*Modeh ani*"[61] when I wake up. I still light those candles. I still fight for joy. That's *emuna.*

6. **Even suffering has meaning.** I don't believe anything is random. If something breaks and needs to be repaired, it might be Hashem sending a blessing to someone else through me. If my plans fall apart, it's His way of protecting me. I've trained myself to look for the lesson in the pain.

7. **My voice matters, and I will use it.** When people ask what I believe, I don't stay quiet. I share books, playlists, websites. I speak up. I want this path to reach the people who need it, especially in places like prisons, where all they've been offered is confusion. This mission isn't just mine; it's bigger than me.

61. Hebrew for "I offer thanks," which are the first words of a short prayer from the Jewish liturgy that is said upon awakening in the morning.

ADDITIONAL INFORMATION

On honoring the seventh day as a Noahide

Many Noahides speak about Shabbat with deep appreciation, but it's important to clarify that within G-d's Torah Law, non-Jews are neither obligated nor permitted to *sanctify* Shabbat, or take on the ritual restrictions of specific actions on Shabbat, as the Jewish people are commanded. The observance of Shabbat as it is commanded in the Torah is a Divine covenantal sign for all Jews, as a result of them being "acquired" by G-d through their miraculous redemption from slavery in Egypt (see *Exodus 15:16* and *Deuteronomy 5:15*), and it is therefore uniquely sanctified for them.[62] The Divine mission for non-Jews that was assigned from the time of Noah after the flood is to be involved every day with making a positive impact on the world around them, while maintaining a higher standard of morality and conduct through adherence to the Noahide Code.

Therefore, when Noahides speak of their correct ways of respectfully and appropriately "honoring the seventh day", they are expressing their acknowledgment of its special significance. They can permissibly do this by choosing to enhance their normal

---

62. See Maharsha's explanation of *Tractate Sanhedrin 58b*, that "Shabbat is like a bride to Israel," and therefore if a non-Jew observes it as a Jew is commanded, that is tantamount to committing adultery on a spiritual level, and adultery is one of the prohibitions within the Seven Noahide Commandments.

activities in more special ways on the seventh day, while at the same time conducting themselves without any ritual restrictions on their actions. For example, this may include preparing a special meal, lighting candles for the evening meal to enhance peace and beauty in the home (without reciting the blessing established for Jews), wearing nicer clothing, spending more quality time with their family or friends, designating some extra time for rest and relaxation, engaging in appropriate Torah study, and/or spending more time in devout prayer.

It is clear that all of those things are just normal, everyday activities, done in a more special way, which could be done on any day. Therefore, they don't violate the prohibition of adding an extra commandment or creating a new religion for one's self. None of them overstep the boundary of the particular observance of a sanctified Shabbat that is commanded upon the Jews. Rather, they are examples of ways that non-Jews may show honor for the significance of G-d's speaking the creation into existence in six days, and then directing His attention to a more spiritual level on the seventh day.

Delving into Torah as a non-Jew

Many Noahides have questions about the boundaries implied by the Torah law that non-Jews are prohibited to "delve deeply" in Torah study *(osek ba'Torah)*, except in matters that are relevant to their observance of their Seven Commandments, while study at a straightforward level is permitted.[63] Some parts of the Oral Torah are in-depth by their very nature, and this includes Talmud, Midrash, authentic Kabbalah, and in-depth explanations of any part of Torah. To learn the guidelines for specific categories of Oral Torah, you can read the chapter on Torah Study for Gentiles in *The Divine Code,* by Rabbi Moshe Weiner.

On finding a Torah-loving mate

Many single Noahides face a unique and heartfelt challenge: finding a spouse who understands and values a Torah-centered life.

I often reflect on the practical wisdom shared by my friend, Jim Long, a long-time Noahide, who found his wife Carol in a way that beautifully aligned with his commitment to Torah. When dating, Jim would invite his date to attend a Torah class with him, carefully observing her reactions. Some women weren't interested, others were indifferent, but Carol, who later became his wife, was curious and engaged. This approach not only showed him who might share his values but also brought Torah into the center of his relationship from the beginning.

While the search for a like-minded partner can be challenging, Jim's example is a wonderful reminder that Torah itself can guide the process.

---

63. See Tractate *Sanhedrin* 59a, which discusses why the prohibition of in-depth Torah study by Jews is not listed explicitly as another one of the Noahide Commandments. It answers that Deut. 33:4 states that, "The Torah that Moses commanded us is a *morasha* /inheritance for the congregation of Jacob." Therefore, if a non-Jew "involves" himself (*osek*) in Torah, which implies in-depth study of Oral Torah for its own sake as Jews are commanded, that is tantamount to stealing Israel's inheritance, and theft is included as one of the prohibitions in the Seven Noahide Commandments. Rather, in-depth Torah study by non-Jews, *if they accept the truth of Torah*, is permitted if it is limited to teachings in the Oral Torah that will serve the practical purpose of making them more expert in their observance of their Seven Noahide Commandments.

    The Talmud on that page also gives an another explanation, that the word in the cited verse can alternatively be read as *morasa* (betrothed), which teaches that the Torah is betrothed to the Jewish people. Therefore, if a non-Jew engages in in-depth Torah study that is not relevant to his practical need to understand observance of his Seven Commandments, that is tantamount to committing adultery on a spiritual level, and adultery is one of the prohibitions within the Seven Noahide Commandments.

Community and fellowship

One of the most essential parts of walking the Noahide path is community and connection. Personal contact with rabbis and teachers has been crucial to my own journey; they are the ones who carry the Torah's wisdom and provide the guidance we need. When face-to-face connection isn't possible, technology like Zoom or Google Meet makes it easier to study and ask questions in real time.

Equally important is the connection with fellow Noahides. This walk can be lonely without others who understand the journey. By sharing experiences, supporting one another, and learning together, we build a strong, vibrant community. With this fellowship, we can remind each other that we are part of something greater, a worldwide effort to bring more goodness, correct spirituality, and the light of Torah into the world.

SOME RECOMMENDED RESOURCES FOR FURTHER LEARNING

Noahide resources

Rabbis and teachers for Noahides

Rabbi Moshe Weiner: Authoritative guide on Torah Laws of Noahide faith and observance. Author of *The Divine Code* and *Seven Gates of Righteous Knowledge.*

Rabbi Tani Burton: Director of Sukkat Shalom B'nei Noach, dedicated to Noahide teaching. SukkatShalom-BneiNoach.com

Rabbi Moshe Perets: President of Noahide Academy of Israel. Coordinator of the Masters Degree in Noahide Theology 3-year program. NoahideAcademy.org

Dr. Michael Schulman: Director of Ask Noah International, a comprehensive resource for Noahide learning. AskNoah.org

Rabbi Tuvia Serber: Teacher for Sukkat Shalom Bnei Noach. SukkatShalom-BneiNoach.com

Websites for Noahide outreach and communities

Asknoah.org: Website of Ask Noah International, offering comprehensive halachic educational resources and guidance for Noahides.

NoahideAcademy.org: Website of the Noahide Academy of Israel (Director, Rabbi Moshe Perets) Educational platform dedicated to teaching the Noahide Laws through courses, guidance, and community.

Dutch Noahide Community (website in Dutch)
DutchNoahideCommunity.nl

Sukkat Shalom Bnei Noah: Community offering classes and fellowship for Noahides. SukkatShalomBneiNoah.com

Books for Noahides

The Divine Code, by Rabbi Moshe Weiner. Detailed halachic guide for the overall Noahide Code (expanded in 2025). Now in the 4th Edition (soft cover) and 5th Edition (hard cover).

Seven Gates of Righteous Knowledge, by Rabbi Moshe Weiner and Dr. Michael Schulman. A concise spiritual and ethical guide for Noahides and all righteous Gentiles.

Prayers, Blessings, Principles of Faith, and Divine Service for Noahides, authorized by Rabbi Moshe Weiner and Rabbi J. Immanuel Schochet. A personal daily resource, available in pocket-size or large-print editions.

Prayers for Noahides: Community and Personal Worship, authorized by Rabbi Moshe Weiner and Rabbi J. Immanuel Schochet. Morning, afternoon and evening prayer services, and additional prayer resources, that can be used by Noahide congregations or individuals.

Go(o)d for You: The Divine Code of 7 Noahide Commandments. An introductory booklet with content from Rabbi Moshe Weiner, Rabbi J. Immanuel Schochet, and other experts, on the sources, meanings and main precepts for each of the Seven Noahide Commandments. Available in print, or free download from Asknoah.org.

To Perfect the World: The Lubavitcher Rebbe's Call to Teach the Noahide Code to All Mankind (2nd Edition). Translated excerpts from the Rebbe's talks during 1982-1992, in which he expounded on the fundamental importance of the Noahide commandments and the urgent need to promote their observance worldwide. Published by Sichos In English.

Emuna and the Noahide: An Emuna-oriented Guidebook for Noahides. (Rabbi Lazer Brody)

Helpful Guide for the Starting Noahide. From the Dutch Noahide Community, publication available in English

Simply Noahide. A Beginner's Guide. (Veronica Port).

Websites of rabbis and teachers for Jewish/Torah content (see Additional Information on p. 199 for guidance)

OutreachJudaism.org: Website of Rabbi Tovia Singer, a renown expert on Torah truths for countering missionary claims.

LazerBeams.com: Rabbi Lazar Brody's inspirational web site that focuses on personal growth and serving G-d through *emuna* (faith).

OhelSara.com: Website of Rabanit K. Sarah Cohen, providing women-focused Torah learning community.

Aish.com: Jewish philosophy, Torah study, and ethical teachings.

Chabad.org: Comprehensive Jewish educational content.

RabbiRichman.com: "Torah for Everyone" – the website for Rabbi Richman's organization, Jerusalem Lights (see the YouTube channel below).

MyJewishLearning.com: an online resource offering accessible articles, guides, and learning materials on Jewish history, culture, beliefs, and daily practice.

TorahAnytime.com: Thousands of Jewish educational lectures.

Hebrew Bible and other Jewish books (available from Amazon.com and other retailers)

The Stone Edition Chumash, published by Artscroll.

The Stone Edition Tanach, published by Artscroll.

Books by Dr. Alan Morinis:
Everyday Holiness: The Jewish Spiritual Path of Mussar.

Every Day Holy Day: 365 Days of Teachings and Practices from the Jewish Tradition of Mussar.

Books by Rabbi Jonathan Sacks:
Morality: Restoring the Common Good in Divided Times. Explores the decline of moral values in modern society and advocates for a return to shared moral principles.

Not in God's Name: Confronting Religious Violence. Addresses the phenomenon of religious extremism and violence, offering insights into how faith can be a force for peace.

Covenant & Conversation. Insightful commentaries on the weekly Torah portions.

Judaism's Life-Changing Ideas: A Weekly Reading of the Jewish Bible. Highlights transformative concepts from the weekly Torah portions.

YouTube videos, podcasts and Instagram

Jerusalem Lights: Torah for Everyone. By Rabbi Chaim Richman. https://www.youtube.com/@jerusalemlights-rabbirichman

History for the Curious: Podcast featuring the dynamic historian and famous tour guide and lecturer, Rabbi Aubrey Hersh. Hosted by Rabbi Mena Reisner. https://rabbiaubreyhersh.podbean.com

Humans4Noah: Jewish Torah lessons for all mankind with Rabbi Raps

FINAL THOUGHT

The NOACH Project is more than a book. It's a movement, and a beacon of light for anyone seeking a life of connection with the Creator. Whether you are just starting this path or continuing to walk it with faith and courage, may this book inspire and support you in your journey.

Leba bat Noah

www.ingramcontent.com/pod-product-compliance
Lightning Source LLC
Chambersburg PA
CBHW031458120626
46545CB00005B/1663
* 9 7 9 8 9 8 5 5 2 2 1 2 9 *